D0777034

CONSTRUCTION NOTES

To Vivian

Thanks for your the
great work in this
beautiful building.

Best for the future.

Wendell Meese Jr.

3/30/2011

CONSTRUCT

Transforming a Campus in Washington, D.C.

ION NOTES

WALLACE MLYNIEC

ON THIS SPOT PRODUCTIONS
GARRETT PARK, MARYLAND

On This Spot books are available through most bookstores. Please direct inquiries to Paul Dickson, On This Spot, PO Box 280, Garrett Park, MD, 20896; newdefiner@aol.com or develyn1@verizon.net. Discounts on bulk quantities of On This Spot books are available to corporations, professional associations, and other organizations. For details and discount information, contact On This Spot. Book design by Jody Billert, Design Literate, Inc.

Printed in the United States of America

ISBN 0-9650998-1-4 (clothbound)
ISBN 0-9650998-2-2 (paperback)

Library of Congress Control Number: 2006921409

First Printing 2006

To my wife Abby Yochelson, librarian par excellence,

and to my children Casey and Emma for their contributions

and patience as both the Georgetown Law Center buildings

and this book came to fruition.

PROLOGUE

In the early months of 2000, my dean at Georgetown Law Center asked me to lead a $61 million construction project designed to erect two buildings that would complete a campus that had begun to develop in 1970. Although I had been on building committees for many years, I was reluctant to lead such a large project. I am a criminal defense lawyer by training and a clinical law professor and academic administrator by profession. I am neither an architect nor an engineer, and I felt ill prepared to lead such an endeavor. My fears were assuaged, however, when I learned that the chief financial officer would handle the construction budget and that I would be permitted to hire my own engineer to give me independent guidance as I negotiated with architects, construction managers, and contractors.

Within a year, my financial officer had left for another job, leaving no replacement, and my engineer had suffered a major heart attack, leaving him in a coma. I learned that his marked-up drawing for security devices, information technology, and audiovisual wiring could not be found and that the contracts for those services had yet to be negotiated. Within weeks of the engineer's heart attack, the architect called me to say he had discovered a design defect in the structural engineering that could conceivably bring the half-finished building crashing to the ground, and that he had ordered all workers out of the building. Three days later a sonic boom from a cloud-hidden airplane found me rushing across the street to the construction site, fully expecting that the building had collapsed.

During the four years I worked on this project, I learned that these experiences, all suggesting lawsuits to a lawyer, were merely part of the day-to-day life of a construction project. Our buildings, beautifully designed and in the end excellently engineered, were subsequently completed on time and under budget, and have gone on to win design and construction awards. The buildings have become the center of campus life and have tied us more firmly to a neighborhood rich in history and with prospects for an even richer future.

TABLE OF CONTENTS

I

INTRODUCTION

On June 1, 2002, officials at Georgetown University Law Center broke ground for two new buildings, the Eric E. Hotung International Law Building and the Georgetown Law Sport and Fitness Center. Designed by Ralph Jackson from the architectural firm of Shepley Bulfinch Richardson and Abbott, and built by Whiting-Turner Contracting Company, these buildings were sited at New Jersey Avenue and F Street, NW. This would place the new buildings in the middle of the Law Center's campus between its Gewirz Residence Hall and its main academic building, McDonough Hall. In an effort to keep the Law Center community informed of our progress, and to minimize the number of complaints that such a project might engender, I began writing e-mails to the students, staff, and faculty.[1] I had the limited goals of making the members of the law school community understand what they were seeing outside their windows, and explaining why the temporary but sometimes significant inconvenience they were experiencing would result in a long-term benefit.

Over time, as I immersed myself in the life of the project, I became fascinated by the interplay between construction design and materials, by the wide and deep knowledge bases of the architects and engineers, and by the skill and judgment that each of the craftsmen brought to the project. Literally tens of thousands of decisions are made on a project of this sort, forcing one to confront the human dimension embodied in these works of stone and steel. Contemplating the present interaction between man and material led me to wonder how that interaction manifested itself over time in an institution whose history is interwoven into the history of a city, and whose campus buildings have occupied several sites in that city during its long history. These musings transformed the informational messages I sent to the community and gave them a new purpose and a new format. Rather than just serving as monthly news alerts, the e-mails began to tell the story of a construction project. The story, however, was not merely a diary of the progress of what came to be known as the Georgetown Campus Completion Project. Instead, I tried to place the awakening of these new buildings in the context of both the story of the workers and materials that make up a modern building and the history of Georgetown Law Center as it developed into an academic

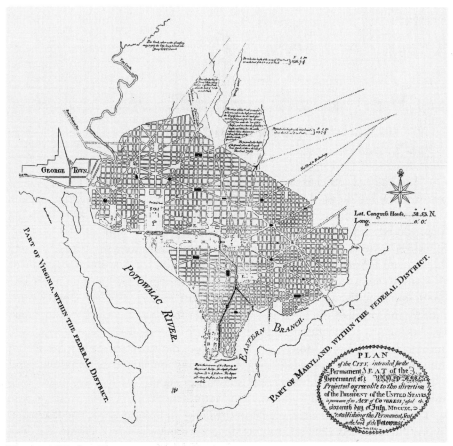

The 1791 L'Enfant Plan
U.S. COAST AND GEODETIC SURVEY

leader among law schools and a civic leader in the old East End neighborhood of Washington, D.C.

I knew a great deal about these stories because of my love for D.C. history, my long association with Georgetown, and a penchant for collecting strange and strangely related bits of information that many would find useless. I have always found them entertaining and, from time to time, others have also. I have also learned a great deal from the wonderful architects and engineers who worked on the Law Center project. People from other disciplines, as well those who, like me, collect unusual bits of information, occasionally provided additional stories and odd facts as these originally unplanned reports became more extensive.

Georgetown University was founded by the famous Jesuit priest, Reverend John Carroll,[2] in 1789, the year that the Articles of Confederation gave way to the United States Constitution. President James Madison ultimately signed its public charter on March 1, 1815, a charter still read at graduation each year to remind its students of the University's roots in this city.[3] The Law Center was founded in 1870, just as Washington, D.C., was emerging from the ravages of the Civil War.[4] The story of Georgetown and its buildings is then, in many ways, the story of Washington, D.C.; but it is less the story of official Washington than it is the story of the land and the city itself, of its swamps and creeks, its streets and parks, and the people who lived in the neighborhoods where Georgetown taught its students.

The life of any city is enhanced by its architecture and the site plan that defines it. Because of Pierre L'Enfant's design for the city, the history of Washington, D.C., cannot fully be told without understanding its architecture and public spaces. L'Enfant's plan, often neglected since his departure, has regained its place as the guiding light to development in Washington, D.C. To fully appreciate the historical and contemporary significance of L'Enfant's plan to the architecture that adorns it, one needs to understand design, materials, and the methods of construction. In my notes to the Law Center community, I tried to capture this synthesis.

This short book, derived from those e-mail postings, is several things. It is a diary of a construction project; it is a limited primer on architectural design and materials; and it is a short history of an academic institution and its place in a city. These three stories combine to define Georgetown University Law Center's campus in the heart of Washington's old East End. As William Faulkner once said, "The past is not dead. In fact, it's not even past." These stories helped to engage an entire academic community not only in the world outside their windows, but in a world outside of windows once built and then torn down. Most of Georgetown's buildings were erected long before the students, faculty, and staff were born and thus, never seen. The people who designed the buildings and those who lived in the surrounding neighborhoods were also gone and for the most part forgotten. The original "Construction Notes" were an architectural and historical reverie of those people, their buildings, and their neighborhoods. Our community found these stories fascinating. I hope you find them just as engaging. To give the reader a sense of time and progress, I have retained the original dates of the Construction Notes postings through out the book.

Pile and lagging board system with tieback secured.
WHITING TURNER CONSTRUCTION PHOTO; BOB CREAMER, PHOTOGRAPHER

II

PILE DRIVING AND LAGGING BOARDS

SEPTEMBER 19, 2002

Since we broke ground in June, the Whiting-Turner Contracting Company has been mobilizing its crew, erecting its construction trailers, studying the construction documents provided by the architects from Shepley Bulfinch Richardson and Abbott and their associate architects at Ellerbe Becket, testing soil samples for composition and contamination, and finalizing bids to subcontractors who will actually perform the thousands of tasks that will culminate in two new buildings and the completion of our East End campus. The East End is a section of the city in the Northwest quadrant bounded roughly by 11th Street on the south, North Capitol Street on the east, and Massachusetts Avenue, Mount Vernon Square and New York Avenue on the north. Our parcel of land at New Jersey Avenue and 1st Street, once home to middle-class families, then leveled for an urban renewal that never came, and most recently a parking lot, will within two years complete the campus of an institution that has its roots deep in the history of Washington, D.C.

Once the site was cleared, construction began in earnest. We are now excavating the pit that will hold the subterranean foundations of the buildings and pounding steel columns into the ground at the edge of the pit to support its walls and the walls of the buildings soon to come. Every construction project of this size requires that piles (steel columns) be driven into the ground and that wooden lagging boards be placed between some of them before construction of the foundations begins. The pile and lagging board system supports the immense weight of the earth that surrounds the excavation pit, preventing the walls from collapsing on the workers and the machinery as the pit grows deeper. Piles also support some of the buildings' foundations.

Although the first round of pile-driving seemed minimally disruptive to our daily academic life, the noise emanating from the pile driver was louder than other construction sounds we heard as the site was being cleared. It will soon be louder still. We are scheduled to begin driving piles adjacent to the Gewirz Residence Hall on Tuesday, September 24. We expect this operation to continue through Thursday, September 26. We will start driving piles at 8:00 a.m. each day and will continue until 4:00 p.m. The noise and vibration will have its greatest effect on the south side of McDonough Hall and the east side of Gewirz Residence Hall. Sleeping in may now become difficult.

The earlier piles we drove supported the earth wall surrounding the excavation pit. The next set of piles will support the actual foundations of the Sport and Fitness Center. The sound of the impact between the steel hammer and the head of the steel pile is explosive. Moreover, the vibration waves emanating from the impact of the hammer and the pile head, as well as from the movement of the earth below as it is displaced by the driven steel toe of the column, will be much more noticeable than that of other pile-driving sessions and may shake the windows of Gewirz. When the pile-driving is complete, we can begin to lay the foundations and the building will begin to rise.

Driven piles or columns are the oldest type of deep foundation support for buildings and bridges. For this section, I rely heavily on Pile Buck, Inc. and the information available on their website.[5] Historically, these columns have been composed of timber, concrete, steel, or a combination of those materials. They have been used throughout the ages across many different cultures as sturdy foundations for bridges, houses, and other structures, especially those built on unsteady land or over water. The Chinese have been using piles for thousands of years. The Romans used wooden piles to support structures over various soils and above water in their far-flung empire. The most famous of the early Roman pile-supported bridges was that built by Julius Caesar over the Rhine during his campaign in Gaul. The oldest, however, was the Pons Sublicius, built before 500 B.C. Knowing the bridge's support capacity proved critical in the early stirrings of the Roman republic. An invading army of the deposed king stormed the bridge only to learn that the combined weight of the soldiers was more than the bridge's support capacity. The bridge collapsed, and the invaders toppled into the river, ending the attack. Wooden piles also support tenth-century structures in Venice. As the water envelops the city today, the thousand-year-old piles continue to support their buildings. It is the rising water more than the sinking buildings that may eventually destroy the city. Early American buildings used wooden piles. In the 1890s, steel-reinforced concrete piles were sometimes used, especially in Chicago; but H-shaped steel piles, like the ones Whiting-Turner is using on our project, have predominated in the construction industry since the early twentieth century.

Piles have always been driven into the ground using some form of a hammer. Early engineers drove piles by hand or by stone drop-hammers falling from small wooden rigs. A steam-driven steel hammer, stronger than the stone hammer and more powerful than hammers dropped from wooden rigs, was developed in 1845 by a Scot named James Naysmith. It came to United States in the 1870s. Piles are driven today by vibratory or impact-vibration hammers supported by crane booms and driven by high-powered motors. They were originally developed by D. D. Barkan in the former Soviet Union in the 1950s. The Russians licensed the technology to the Japanese, who made significant modifications and exported the technology around the world. While the rest of the world was using vibratory or impact-vibration hammers initially designed by Russian or Japanese engineers, Americans developed their own style of hammers after 1969. They have now been adopted across the globe.

Many factors are taken into consideration before piles are driven, irrespective of whether they provide foundation or soil support. Because the surface soil is usually soft or sandy and unable to support a building, piles are used to transfer the weight of a building to the subsurface level which is deeper, more compact, and thus, more stable and capable of supporting a structure. Geotechnical engineers test the soil to determine an appropriate pile capacity, that is, how much weight the piles can support at different depths without settling deeper into the ground. The soil's penetration resistance is measured by conducting a subsurface investigation using either the Standard Penetration Test (SPT) or the Cone Penetration Test (CPT). We used the SPT, developed in the United States around 1925.[6]

Soil is tested by sending a relatively simple and inexpensive, but rugged, probe into pre- bored holes in the ground. In our case, we used a two-inch-diameter, split-barrel sampler driven by a 140-pound hammer falling thirty inches. The number of blows required to drive the sampler through a twelve-inch interval is termed the Standard Penetration Test (SPT) value and is indicated for each sample in the boring logs. The number of blows to the hammer over a specific interval are counted, resulting in a "blow count." Comparing the number of blows to a known standard determines the composition of the soil at various levels. Knowing the composition helps the engineer determine how deep the foundation piles must be driven to support the weight of the building, the people and furniture that occupy it, and the pressure caused by natural forces such as wind and gravity.

The piles we are driving for the foundation wall closest to the Gewirz Residence Hall must extend deep below the surface soil, since it is essentially backfill dumped in after the construction of the Gewirz Residence Hall. Because the backfill is soft and not compacted, the concrete foundation walls for the Sport and Fitness Building would sink, crack the foundations, and even endanger the building if the pile foundations did not reach down to the compacted earth. In our case, the foundation piles will have to be driven between fifty and eighty feet into the soil to meet the design requirements. Because steel piles are seldom fabricated longer than forty feet in length, sections will have to be welded together to reach those depths.

Most of the excavation pit is now surrounded by steel piles that were driven thirty feet into the ground into soil that was solid and compacted over many years. (See photo on page 4.) The piles are connected by wooden lagging boards. Lagging boards are horizontal wooden boards that are placed in between steel vertical piles to help retain the walls of the pit as the excavation proceeds downward. Tiebacks are placed through the lagging boards at ten- to twelve-foot intervals around the edge of the excavation pit to help hold back the earth behind the lagging boards. Tiebacks are essentially steel cables. They are inserted into holes that were previously drilled laterally into the soil behind the sheeting wall. Grout is then forced into the holes to secure the cables. Finally, the tieback is fastened to the lagging boards and tightened. The length of the tieback is based on loads and soil characteristics. They are then anchored to either the vertical steel piles or to steel walers, which are horizontal steel beams spanning multiple piles. Once the grout has sufficiently cured, the tiebacks are tensioned to provide additional support for the excavation walls.[7] This process is repeated every ten to twelve feet down until the proper subgrade is reached. The combination of piles, lagging boards, and tiebacks hold back the walls of the excavated site so that they do not collapse as we move into the next phase of construction.

As you can imagine, impact hammers slamming down from the top of cranes, striking steel columns hard enough and frequently enough to drive them eighty feet into the ground are noisy and annoying, especially if you are studying or trying to teach a class. We are trying to accommodate some of the events that are taking place at the Law Center this week but we will not always be successful. Please bear with us.

III

TOWER CRANE

OCTOBER 18, 2002

There are only four more foundation piles to drive. Barring some unforeseen problem, we should finish tomorrow. Tomorrow will also mark another milestone in our construction project as we will complete the mass excavation of the site. Although excavation will continue in a few small areas, we will have reached the subgrade level upon which the building will stand.

The next exciting part of the project will be the construction of a tower crane that will rise higher than the Gewirz Residence Hall. If you loved playing with Legos, Tinker Toys, or Erector Sets as a kid (or still do), you will love this stage of the project. The concrete foundation forms for the crane are almost in place, and the crane itself will begin to rise on Tuesday. Tower cranes are visible all across our city's skyline. These lopsided T-shaped steel structures provide both stability and strength to lift heavy building materials such as concrete and steel within a confined area. Although mobile cranes can serve the same purposes, the restricted nature of urban building sites makes their use impractical.

Tower cranes are composed of several distinct parts.[8] (See photo on page 10.) The base is bolted to a concrete pad that supports the crane. The mast is the large vertical section that connects to the base and rises to its assigned height. On top of the mast is the slewing unit, which holds the gears and the motor that permits the crane to rotate to the position of the lift or the deposit. Three parts sit above the slewing unit. The horizontal working arm, or jib, carries the load horizontally by way of a trolley so that it can be placed at any spot along the length of the jib. The shorter machinery arm contains the crane's electronics, the motors which lift the load, and more importantly, the counterweights which serve to balance the load and prevent the crane from toppling over while carrying materials. The crane's operator sits in a cab perched high upon the tower, coordinating the gears and cables so that the loads are safely raised from one area of the site and deposited in another. Since he has to climb to the top of the crane to reach his cab, he usually remains in the cab atop the crane for his entire shift.

It takes several days to assemble a tower crane. First, anchor bolts are embedded in the concrete slab and attached to the base section of the crane. Some

The 200-foot, flag-topped tower crane, work horse of the project
WHITING TURNER CONSTRUCTION PHOTO; BOB CREAMER, PHOTOGRAPHER

cranes, especially those in taller buildings, "grow" as a unit. In that case, the two horizontal portions of the "T" are constructed by smaller mobile cranes and mounted onto the slewing unit. The whole assembly is then placed as a single unit onto a section of the tower crane's mast. Once the horizontal pieces are in place, counterweights are added to one side to balance the heavy loads that the tower crane will soon be lifting. Now the tower is ready to rise. A climbing frame is inserted between the top of the mast section and the slewing unit. Slowly, hydraulic lifts in the climbing frame raise the top part of the crane and provide a space to add another mast segment. The horizontal arm lifts a mast segment into the opening. Thus, the tower crane has grown itself by one mast segment. The process repeats itself until the tower crane reaches the desired height.[9]

The construction of our crane will be much simpler. It will sit on a base built from 140 cubic yards of concrete. The mast will be erected to its maximum height by workers positioning sections lifted into place one after the other by a mobile crane. Once the mast is built, mobile cranes will lift the slewing unit, jib, machinery, and counterweights to the top, where they will be assembled. Unsupported tower cranes can rise to a height of 265 feet. In larger buildings, the crane is secured to a core in the building so that it can grow even higher. Our tower crane will reach a height of two hundred feet. For reference, the Washington Monument rises to about 555 feet, and the dome of the U.S. Capitol is about 288 feet from the ground. Crane jibs can reach up to 230 feet in length. The jib on our crane will be 220 feet long. At its tip, it will be able to lift twelve thousand pounds. At a position close to the cab, it can lift thirty-five thousand pounds. Its thirty-thousand-pound counterweight will keep it from tipping when it lifts and moves loads. Counterweights on larger cranes may reach forty thousand pounds, or twenty tons. Once built, our crane will be used to pour concrete (two cubic yards per bucket is typical), lift formwork, plywood, and framing lumber, set reinforcing steel, unload material from trucks, and move that material to the building decks or floors as they are being formed and poured. It may also be used to set some of the structural steel and, of course, to fly the flag.

During the month of October, activity will increase, and more workers will occupy the site. We will be creating the cement footings for the buildings and preparing to erect the foundation walls. We will hear the sound of trucks and a generator, but nothing involving the high decibels and pounding that have recently marked our days. It will be the sight of the tower crane, however, graceful yet sturdy, stable yet dynamic, that signals to the Law Center community and to our neighbors that we are building in earnest, that our structures are rising with our aspirations, and that the dreams of our founders are coming to fruition. Our intentions will be visible not only from the ground, but from the tops of other cranes around the city, all rising to celebrate the renaissance of Washington, D.C.

The excavation pit uncovered three distinct layers of soil and sediment
WHITING TURNER CONSTRUCTION PHOTO; BOB CREAMER, PHOTOGRAPHER

IV

GEOLOGY

NOVEMBER 1, 2002

For the past few weeks, we have been pouring concrete foundations and forming and pouring concrete columns. Wall forms and reinforcing steel are being set to pour the perimeter foundation wall. Indeed, one section of the wall has already been poured.

If you look into the excavation pit, you can get some sense of the geology of this area. Geologically speaking, the Law Center is in the Coastal Plain, formed millions of years ago by ancient oceans, sweeping down along a region of metamorphic rock called the Piedmont.[10] The fall line of the Piedmont, where it meets the coastal plain, is located to our north. Three layers of deposits appear in the excavation site: a thin upper layer of soil, broken bricks, and other evidence of human occupation; a middle layer, pink to brown in color, composed of mostly clay that is evidence of a swamp that covered much of this area well into the 1800s; and then sand, of a quality usually found around moving water. The top layer reflects the presence of the white man, beginning around 1800. Although Indians roamed this land, they did not form permanent settlements here. The second layer reflects the swamps that began to form in this area millions of years ago as waters flooded and receded, destroying forms of animal life and vegetation, and then leaving them to decay. The top two layers of soil in our pit are thus easily understood. The lowest layer, however, raises the question of how this sand came to be here, and why it is mixed with larger rocks that are more commonly found one hundred miles away.

A clue comes from some of the rocks and pebbles one finds mixed in with the sand. The smaller rounded quartz pebbles suggest moving water. Their roundness suggests that they were formed by a river, tumbling them over and over, rather than by the ebb and flow of ocean waves which flatten the stones as it polishes them. The larger cobbles are of a kind usually found around Hancock, Maryland, a region to our north and west, that suggests that the larger rocks were brought here by a powerful moving force. Sandstone rocks like this were also found in the 1890s during excavations in Alexandria, Virginia.

During the period when the glaciers covered Pennsylvania, this region endured much rain because of climatic upheaval.[11] Many swift-moving rivers, caused by the rain and the melting glaciers, covered the coastal plain, carving deep channels. As the rains gradually ended and the water receded, its power diminished. The remaining deep channels formed many rivers and creeks. Remnants of those rivers remain, some wide and flowing like the Potomac and the Anacostia, some merely hidden meanders or trickling streams like Goose Creek, also called Tiber Creek,[12] which flowed in this area until the early 1900s. The area where the water receded slowly expanded the swamp. The swamp remained late into the 1800s and gave rise to this neighborhood's nickname, Swampoodle.[13]

But, back to the sand: it is difficult to actually date a piece of sand, but since it was deposited during the era of the glaciers, one can guess it is between 10,000 and 1 million years old, although some of it may even be older. This may seem an imprecise measurement, but in geologic time it is less than a heartbeat. The earliest evidence of preserved life in the D.C. area, Cretaceous period plants and animals, are about 100 million years old.[14] The rocky Piedmont began to form at least 400 million years ago.[15]

Looking at our rising new buildings, surrounded by signs of life that are less than one hundred years old, hardly reminds us of what has happened here before the dawn of man. And yet, the evidence of an ancient earth, and people from another time, impact the work we do. Our time will pass too, but we must make the best of it.

By the way, we have lost a few work days, and probably a few grains of sand, because of the great amount of rain that has swept this area of late. As a result, we will need to catch up. Crews will be arriving at seven in the morning and will be working beyond their usual 3:30 p.m. shift end for the next few weeks. You will also see workmen here on Saturdays. Noise levels will remain the same for the next few weeks.

V

DINOSAURS AND INDIANS

NOVEMBER 15, 2002

We have reached the point in the construction project where one can begin to see the outline of the Hotung Building. Viewed from the top of Gewirz, the foundation walls give a sense of the Hotung Building's perimeter. On the F Street side, you can see the gentle curve of the north wall, an architectural lagniappe that beckons to, but does not replicate, the drum-shaped entrances and rotundas of our other buildings. To the west, you can see where the wall will open to permit access at the parking level into the Sport and Fitness Center. To the north again, we have poured the floor slab for one of the mechanical rooms. The top of the columns throughout the excavation pit show where the slab for the first floor will begin.

We have essentially completed the excavation. The dimensions of the excavation are quite impressive. The pit is 280 feet long and 232 feet wide. Its deepest point is twenty-three feet below the street. We removed 945,000 cubic feet of dirt. Since each cubic foot of dirt weighs about 133 pounds, we removed 125,685,000 pounds of soil.

Recognizing that we were removing a large amount of dirt, several people have asked me whether we discovered any Native American artifacts or fossils on the site. The answer is no. If we had, construction would have had to stop while archeologists and anthropologists combed the site for remnants of the past. Nonetheless, both Native Americans and dinosaurs inhabited this area at one time. The earliest sighting of Native Americans by Europeans occurred in 1608 when Captain John Smith saw members of the Powhatan band on the Potomac River just north of what is now Georgetown.[16] Many of the Nacosin Indians, of Algonquin lineage, lived on the banks of the Anacostia River in a large village called Nacotchtank. The village stretched from near Bladensburg, Maryland, to the confluence of the Anacostia and Potomac rivers. Another band lived in a smaller village called Tahoga in what is now Georgetown. The closest village to the Law Center was at 2nd and Duddington Streets, SE, just south of the House office buildings and near Garfield Park. These bands were farmers and

Concrete foundations where the Capitalasaurus once roamed
WHITING TURNER CONSTRUCTION PHOTO; BOB CREAMER, PHOTOGRAPHER

fishermen, but they also hunted along the Tiber or Goose Creek and in the swamps that covered our land. Nacotchtank disappeared from European records in the early 1630s as the villagers moved further down river to a spot near Nanjemoy, Maryland. It was among the bands living along the Potomac that the Jesuit missionaries began their work in 1639.[17] The villages are all long gone, but the presence of their inhabitants is remembered in the name Anacostia, both the river and the section of the city, an English corruption of the name Nacosin.

As for dinosaurs, they too inhabited this area, but little evidence remains in the Coastal Plain because of the floods during the glacial era. Nonetheless, D.C. Code 1-161 designates the Capitalasaurus as the official dinosaur of the District of Columbia. Fossil remains from this dinosaur were discovered in 1898 at 1ˢᵗ and F Streets, SE, near the site of that old Native American village. The dinosaur was 110 million years old and may have been an ancestor of Tyrannosaurus rex.[18] Like so many other things in D.C., it is unique in that no other fossil like it has ever been found in the world.

In the last two messages, I have tried to give some sense of our neighborhood's distant past. In the next, I will try to give you some sense of its future.

VI

THE FUTURE OF THE NEIGHBORHOOD

DECEMBER 6, 2002

Foundation work for both buildings continues. All of the columns and wall footings for the Hotung Building are complete. We have begun to lay the concrete slab on grade that will become the garage floor and an elevated slab that will become the first floor. You can begin to see the outline of the Sport and Fitness Center as well. Construction of foundation walls and columns will soon be completed. The small hill to the rear of the lot marks the site of the lap pool. Tons of concrete have been poured into the site, and through it all, the Tower Crane has been the workhorse of our efforts.

The view from the top of the Tower Crane, three stories higher than Gewirz, is both impressive and instructive. To the north, one can see the fall line of the Piedmont, running through Meridian Hill Park.[19] To the east, train lines emanate from Union Station, which was designed by Daniel Burnham[20] in the early 1900s to consolidate the railroad terminals in D.C. Built as part of the City Beautiful movement at the turn of the century, Union Station eliminated the train tracks and a station from the base of the Capitol, permitting an unimpeded expanse on what is now the National Mall.[21] To the south, the gently rising banks of the Anacostia River and the Potomac River watershed mark the edge of the Coastal Plain as it runs down to the Chesapeake Bay. In between is the marvelous Federal City laid out by Pierre L'Enfant in 1791.[22]

From this high vantage point, the future of Washington, D.C. appears along with its past. No fewer than twenty-three other tower cranes are visible from the top of ours. They are building the modern city envisioned by the District's Downtown Action Agenda.[23] The Agenda calls for 3,500 new housing units, 330,000 square feet of new retail space, 850 new theater seats, fourteen new movie screens, and three new museums, all to be opened by December 2004. Much of this construction will occur in or near our neighborhood and will transform life at the Law Center. For example, apartments are now under construction at three locations between the Law Center and Fifth Street, NW, along Massachusetts Avenue. Over four hundred additional apartments and town houses, a grocery store, other retail outlets, and a multi-screen movie theater are planned for the corner of Fifth and K Streets, NW. Across the street from us at the triangle park, the National Association of Realtors plans to build a dramatically designed, all-glass office building. It is scheduled to open around the same time as our buildings in 2004.[24] This vibrant cityscape will fulfill dreams of Georgetown Law School's former Dean Paul Dean and his colleagues in 1971, when McDonough Hall opened and Georgetown became the pioneer developer in this neighborhood. Although relations between towns and educational institutions are often rocky, D.C. has always recognized that our continued commitment to and investment in this neighborhood has been a critical factor to its now-emerging renaissance. The assistance of our City Councilwoman Sharon Ambrose and Council Chair Linda Cropp were invaluable as we prepared our plans for the buildings.

VII

CONCRETE

JANUARY 10, 2003

Welcome back. While you were celebrating your holidays, the Whiting-Turner construction crews were very busy. We have finished pouring most of the foundation walls for both buildings, so their outlines are now completely discernible when viewed from the twelfth floor of Gewirz. We have poured the entire garage deck and much of the first-floor deck. The mound of dirt in the rear center of the Sport and Fitness Center marks the pool area; the rising columns in the front show the curve of the two-story glass curtain wall. From the east door of Gewirz, you can now see how the slope of the land gives us a first-floor entrance to the Hotung Building and a second-floor entrance to the Sport and Fitness Center. Columns are now rising and forms are being built to pour the second floor.

The Hotung Building will be constructed entirely from concrete and masonry while the Sport and Fitness Center will have a steel frame and a masonry and glass exterior. All of the decks and columns for both buildings, however, are built from reinforced concrete. For this Construction Note, I mainly referenced the "concrete" and "building construction" entries of the *Encyclopedia Britannica*.[25] Concrete is simply a mixture of gravel, pebbles, broken stone, sand, water, and cement, which hardens into a water- and fire-resistant solid of great compressive strength. Despite its simplicity, concrete's development significantly altered the way large buildings and major public structures are built. Clay was one of the earliest bonding substances. The Assyrians and Babylonians used it to erect their buildings, but it was not very durable and thus, their buildings are lost in antiquity. The ancient Egyptians developed a bonding material more closely resembling modern concrete. They used lime and gypsum as binders and used this concrete extensively. It was the Romans, however, who dramatically expanded architectural methods by using a stronger concrete made from volcanic ash cement. With this form of concrete and a greater understanding of compression, Roman architects were able to develop domes, arches and vaults to cover large spaces, and sturdy foundations for large public buildings, bridges, and sewers. Some of the earliest surviving examples of Roman buildings made with concrete are the Temple of Sybil, built at Tivoli in the first century B.C., and the walls of

Concrete structure of the Hotung Building
WHITING TURNER CONSTRUCTION PHOTO; BOB CREAMER, PHOTOGRAPHER

the Camp of the Praetorian Guard, built in Rome in 21 A.D. The Emperor Nero also used concrete to build an octagonal domed vault in the Golden House, built in 68 A.D. Perhaps if he had used more concrete, less of Rome would have burned while he fiddled.

The use of concrete declined in the Middle Ages but was revived in 1824 with the development of Portland cement by Joseph Aspdin. Portland cement, named after the stone found on the Isle of Portland off the coast of Britain, is made by heating a combination of limestone and clay containing oxides of calcium, iron, aluminum, and silicon, and then pulverizing the resultant fused matter. Concrete made with Portland cement produced stronger bonds than former concretes, thus permitting the construction of larger buildings. In 1867, Joseph Monier, a French gardener, patented a method of strengthening thin concrete flowerpots by embedding iron wire into the concrete. This process ultimately led to the development of reinforced concrete. By the end of the century, the notion of reinforcing concrete with iron bars to create a great tensile strength to complement its compressive strength, had become common. As a result, the stone edifice gave way to the less expensive reinforced concrete and brick buildings.

The architectural value of reinforced concrete cannot be underestimated. It is inexpensive and easy to obtain when compared to the quarried stone that was used for foundations and structures through the early nineteenth century. It has great load-carrying capacity and thus can support large structures. For example, in our buildings, we are pouring the concrete to a compressive strength of 3,000 pounds per square inch in the footings and 4,000 pounds per square inch in the floors and columns. That means a six-inch by twelve-inch test cylinder will withstand over 100,000 pounds of pressure without crumbling. Although the calculations become complicated for standing buildings because of floor spans and tensile strength ratios, the floors in our buildings are built to support 250 pounds of weight per square foot. Finally, because concrete is applied in a liquid form, it allows for greater architectural expression than some other materials. The cylindrical drum-shaped entrances of the Williams Library, the Gewirz Residence Hall, and the East Wing of McDonough were all formed with precast concrete. The curved foundation in the north end of the Hotung Building was poured into forms on site. Although these architectural features could be obtained with other substances, they are easier to form with concrete.

To obtain all of these advantages, however, concrete must be poured carefully and in good weather. Excess water in the mixture and cold and hot weather during the curing period affect the strength and drying time of concrete. Although you may see workers walking on the surface of a concrete floor within a couple of hours after it is poured, it continues to cure at high but decreasing internal temperatures for several days. For many months after that, the concrete remains chemically active inside, growing stronger with the passage of time.

Our concrete work has produced some interesting facts. By the time we are finished, we will have poured 11,600 cubic yards (1,300 truckloads) of concrete. If the trucks were lined up end to end, they would stretch six and one-half miles. The concrete is reinforced by 1,350,000 linear feet of reinforced steel bars called rebar. Lined up end to end, the rebar would stretch over 250 miles.

The American Colonization Building, designed by J. Crawford Neilson
THE HISTORICAL SOCIETY OF WASHINGTON, D.C.

VIII

THE LAW CENTER'S FIRST HOME

JANUARY 31, 2003

The Hotung Building continues to rise. The second-floor deck is completely poured and columns are now being erected to support the third floor. Most of the second-floor deck of the Sport and Fitness Center has also been poured. To the rear, we await the slabs for the swimming pool.

Some of you have asked about the large concrete pipe along the edge of the pool area. The complexity of erecting two completely different buildings which connect, and then connect again to a third building, the Gewirz Residence Hall, cannot be underestimated. Given the ceiling height restrictions in the garage and our design for the whirlpools in the locker rooms, it is not possible to hang exhaust ductwork for the garage from its ceiling. Thus, the reinforced concrete pipe serves as the exhaust ductwork for the garage. The pipe is forty-eight inches in diameter and weighs about 80,000 pounds. The size is necessary to handle the large volume of air that must be removed from the parking areas of the two buildings. The strength and resulting weight are necessary to support the weight of the backfill and pool deck directly above it.

With the completion of the Hotung Building and the Sport and Fitness Center, the Law Center campus will have five buildings on 6.7 acres of land. When the law school was founded in 1870, few people could have anticipated such a campus. Indeed, when the national government moved to the District in 1800, many people believed that the city would be nothing more than an unpleasant backwater, where leaders of the states would have to go periodically to do the business of the federal government. Although there were high hopes for economic development, it was slow in coming to the city due to shortages of skilled labor. Political strife between the Democrats and Federalists still threatened the very existence of the Union. Moreover, relocation of the Capital to another city was actively on the Congressional agenda until 1810, returned to it after the War of 1812, and returned yet again after the Civil War.[26] Nonetheless, the District grew in fits and starts, with poverty, filth, and violence living alongside great wealth, grand and elegant homes, and an increasing number of noble public buildings.[27]

The real transformation of Washington from a swampy, Southern town into what would become a city of classic urban design and proportion began in 1870. For the next three years, until the nationwide depression of 1873, Alexander "Boss" Shepherd[28] (thus, the Shepherd Park neighborhood) directed a massive public works project to turn the miles of dirt roads into brick, wooden, and paved streets and sidewalks lined with trees and gas lamps, and to transform the fetid, disease-filled swamps, creeks, and canals into a modern sewer system. Unfortunately, he did not have enough money to pay the bill, a sad fact discovered only after the depression took hold. Shepherd was ultimately driven out of town by his political enemies in 1876 and moved to Mexico, but he returned to a triumphant parade in his honor in 1887.[29] In the early 1900s, a statue of him was placed in front of the District Building.[30]

In that same decade, Georgetown Law School took its bold, yet tentative, first steps to becoming an institution of academic and professional excellence, worthy of its place in our now vibrant and powerful national city. The law school's founding in 1870 was bold because only thirty one other law schools existed at that time, only one of which, Notre Dame, was affiliated with a Catholic university.[31] In fact, only nine states even required a period of study as a precursor to the practice of law. The school's founding was tentative because its success was far from guaranteed. It had to compete with Columbian University (now George Washington University) for students. Four years after its founding, the entire faculty either resigned or was "restructured." While the reasons remain hidden to history, the parting was not pleasant.[32] Moreover, the city's economic downturn in 1873 caused enrollment to drop to twenty-four students by 1877.[33]

The Georgetown Law Department's first home during this turbulent decade was located in the heart of the city at 4½ Street and Pennsylvania Avenue NW, midway between the Capitol Building and the President's House. Running south from the old City Hall (now 451 Indiana Avenue, NW, and soon to be the home of the D.C. Court of Appeals), 4½ Street was later renamed John Marshall Place and more recently became the plaza of John Marshall Park. Although there was ample land on the main campus to house the new law school, Georgetown chose, for reasons that remain compelling today, to locate its first home amidst the people, the courts, the Congress, and the other pillars of the recently preserved Union.[34]

Had Pierre L'Enfant witnessed the architectural activity between the Capitol and the President's House at that time, he might have been amazed. Lore suggests that L'Enfant had envisioned the Federal District growing eastward from Jenkins Hill, the site of the Capitol, rather than westward.[35] There the land was higher and thus, less swampy. Moreover, the port at the confluence of the Anacostia and Potomac Rivers were deeper than those between old Georgetown and the Capitol. Nonetheless, by 1870, the commercial and residential areas of the city were firmly entrenched between the White House and the Capitol.

The law school rented space in a building designed in 1860 by J. Crawford Neilson[36] and owned by the American Colonization Society. (See photo on page 24.) This building exhibits brick masonry, concentric semi-circular arches set within one another, deeply recessed windows, a classic revival base and cornice, and a beltcourse, all characteristic of Romanesque Revival architecture. Interestingly, it anticipates the architectural era of "Richardson Romanesque," which began ten years later. "Richardsonian Romanesque" is named for Henry H. Richardson, a founding partner of our current design firm, Shepley Bulfinch Richardson and Abbott.[37]

The American Colonization Society, founded in 1817 by Supreme Court Justice Bushrod Washington,[38] was dedicated to resettling free blacks in Africa. Beginning during the presidency of James Monroe in 1822, the Society eventually transported more than 6,000 African American men and women, along with missionaries and teachers, to Liberia and to an adjacent colony on the West African coast called Maryland,[39] where they developed towns and trades and founded the first democracy on the African continent. Rents from the tenants in the Society Hall, Georgetown's included, helped to support those activities. The law school remained a tenant until 1872, when it moved to the Old Washington Seminary. The Colonization Society Hall remained standing until around 1930 when it was demolished as Constitution Avenue was cut through from 6th Street to Pennsylvania Avenue, NW. The land remained vacant until the National Gallery of Art, designed by John Russell Pope,[40] was built between 1937 and 1941. If my eyes serve me well, the building would have stood in the gardens at the east end of the Art Gallery's West Wing, stretching into the plaza between the Pope building and the East Wing designed by I.M. Pei.[41]

Reinforced steel bars supporting concrete columns and walls
WHITING TURNER CONSTRUCTION PHOTO; BOB CREAMER, PHOTOGRAPHER

IX

CONCRETE REDUX

FEBRUARY 21, 2003

The Blizzard of February 2003,[42] though magnificent and mighty, was an unwelcome surprise for our project. We had hoped to get a little ahead of schedule during the Presidents' Day break. Instead, our crews were idle on Monday and spent most of Tuesday and Wednesday digging equipment and tools out from under the snow and clearing forms so that the concrete pours could continue. When creating a construction schedule, we expect that a number of snow and rain days will occur during the life of a project and extend the completion date to account for the losses. So despite this and the other weather delays we have experienced during this unusual Washington winter, the completion date remains the same.

When the site is viewed from the twelfth floor of Gewirz, one can see that the concrete slab on the third floor of the Hotung Building is now complete, and columns are rising to support the fourth floor. One small section of the Sport and Fitness Center's south foundation wall remains unfinished, but we have begun to pour the largest single concrete slab of the project, the second floor of the Sport and Fitness Center. We will pour 570 cubic yards of concrete into the forms.

Given the storm and the cold weather, several people have asked how we can continue to pour concrete. As I mentioned in a previous note, the chemical reaction within the concrete generates heat. On very large projects, such as the new Woodrow Wilson Bridge across the Potomac River, the internal temperature of the concrete foundations will rise to 145 degrees Fahrenheit while curing.[43] Although the internal heat in our concrete will be much lower, we must still prevent heat from escaping too rapidly when the cold or freezing temperatures surround the outer edges of the slabs and columns. If the core and outer temperatures of the concrete cannot be maintained within 35 degrees of each other, the concrete will crack or weaken.

To ensure the structural integrity of the building, the concrete arrives at the site bearing a temperature of about 65 degrees. For about three hours before the pour, eight to ten propane heaters are set beneath the forms upon which the concrete will be poured. These heaters produce about 250,000 BTUs of energy and raise the temperature under the slab to about 75 or 80 degrees. The heaters also warm the reinforcing steel rods so that the concrete does not freeze immediately when it comes in contact with the rebar. After the pour, insulated blankets are placed over the slab or around the column while the heaters continue to fire for at least seventy-two hours, the critical period for curing the concrete. During the cure, thermometers are kept between the blankets and the concrete slab to monitor the temperature and keep it constant.

The day after the pour, a core is drilled into the slab and a thermometer is inserted in the slab itself. If the temperature of the concrete drops below or rises above about 60 degrees, the heaters are adjusted. Finally, a sample of each pour is saved in a separate testing core. Those cores are tested by Whiting-Turner and also by our own independent testing company to ensure that the concrete is maintained at a proper temperature and that the structural integrity of the building is preserved.

Concrete is an amazing substance. It is simple, yet complex; rugged, yet elegant. Its place in architectural history and in the rise of urban culture is subtle but also dominant. It is the tool of an engineer, for highways, bridges, flyovers, and foundations; it is the art of the architect, in itself or as an element of design.

The Old Washington Seminary, Georgetown Law Center's second home
GEORGETOWN LAW CENTER ARCHIVE

X

THE LAW CENTER'S SECOND HOME

MARCH 14, 2003

We continue to pour concrete as we await the arrival of structural steel for the Sport and Fitness Center. The fifth floor of Hotung will be completed on Monday and the column forms for the sixth and final floor are now being poured. We begin several new phases of construction this coming week. The last section of the foundation wall is poured, the subsurface walls are waterproofed, and the pit is backfilled, all preliminary to framing and pouring the lap pool. Moreover, leveling plates are set at the column anchor bolt locations in the Sport and Fitness Center, anticipating the arrival of the steel which will form its structural frame. We will also begin demolition of the two townhouses behind Gewirz. We have placed a second web-camera on the Gewirz building to give a more complete look at the project.

As new construction continues, we continue the architectural story of the former, and now lost, buildings of the Law Center. When the Territory of Columbia was founded, Washington City, Georgetown, and Alexandria were separate cities within two counties in the Territory. As the first two decades of the 1800s unfolded, citizens in Washington City lived mainly around Pennsylvania Avenue west of the Capitol, seldom residing north of F Street. Another small cluster lived near the port on Capitol Hill. Maps of our current neighborhood, bounded by North Capitol Street, 2nd Street, D Street, and Massachusetts Avenue, show few buildings before 1850. Even when the Law School was founded in 1870, the land to the east and north of our present site remained rural and sparsely settled, due in part to the swamps surrounding the Tiber Creek. Between 1870 and 1900, however, development began and people could be found living and working here. Despite the increasing activity in the neighborhood after the Civil War, a century would pass before Georgetown Law Center would leave the west edge of the East End and migrate to its current neighborhood on the east edge.

The law school's second home was again in rented space, this time in the Old Washington Seminary. Like that of its first home, this site evokes architectural and historical reverie. In 1792, St. Patrick's became the first Catholic congregation in Washington City.[44] Within St. Patrick's little wooden church at 9th and F

Streets, NW, worshipped the Irish stonemasons who came to America to build the Federal City, as well as all the prominent Catholics in the city, including Pierre L'Enfant. By 1809, the congregation had outgrown its first church and a second one was built on the southwest portion of the same block. James Hoban,[45] the Irish-born architect and church parishioner who designed the President's House may have also designed St. Patrick's second church, but there is no certainty to that claim. St. Patrick's second church was the first building in Washington City erected in the Gothic Revival style which was popular in England at the time. As can be seen at the left side of the photograph (page 30), the architect designed a simple brick building with arched peaks and slender lancet windows and doors characteristic of Gothic Revival architecture. If Hoban built the church, he may also have designed the building next to it, a building destined to become the Washington Seminary and, ultimately, the Georgetown Law School's second home. The building appears to be connected to St. Patrick's and was built with the same brick. Its foundation stone bore the date of 1815, only a year before St. Patrick's completed an addition to the east side of the church. It is noteworthy also that Hoban owned the Seminary land prior to construction. In a maneuver common to the time in Washington and still common today, he purchased the land for five pounds sterling (about $125) and sold it ninety days later to St. Patrick's for $500, a considerable profit in those days. St. Patrick's then sold the land to the Jesuits for $1.00.[46]

Although connected to St. Patrick's Church, the Washington Seminary building was not constructed in the Gothic Revival style. It is rectangular in shape, has three stories and an attic, alternating six-pane over six-pane and nine-pane over nine-pane windows, and a low-hipped roof with dormers, all of which place it clearly in the Federal style that supplanted Georgian architecture in America after the Revolutionary War. It does not, however, have the decorative elements of high Federal architecture and was essentially a utilitarian building.

Gothic Revival architecture did not achieve much popularity in American civic architecture except in religious buildings. Some say the democratic impulses of the new nation rebelled against both English and clerical motifs. St. Patrick's and the Washington Seminary, however, did have lasting legacies. The priests of St. Patrick's were friends of presidents and of the founding families of the old Maryland and Virginia colonies. They were active in the civic affairs of the new nation and prodigious purveyors of education and charity. In addition to the Washington Seminary, they were involved in the founding of St. Vincent's Orphanage and day school, St. Joseph's School for Women (which became the Convent and Academy of the Visitation), St. Joseph's Male Orphan Asylum and day school, and St. John's College High School.[47]

By 1865, the Gothic Revival church began to deteriorate due to the several springs and streams that ran beneath the property. After a last mass was said there in 1870, St. Patrick's demolished the church, developed the land for commercial purposes, and collected rent. Some of the facades of those buildings still stand although the site is currently being redeveloped. Construction began on a third church at the corner of 10th and G Streets, NW, in 1872. Despite financial setbacks caused by the depression of 1873, the church was completed in 1884. Designed by New York architect Lawrence J. O'Connor[48] in the Victorian Gothic Revival style, it remains today in its original location. St. Patrick's continues to function as a parish and is considered to be the "Mother Church" of Catholic Washington.

The Washington Seminary, founded by Reverend Anthony Kohlman in 1821, was one of the first educational institutions in the old Washington City.[49] The Jesuits originally planned to use the building as a House for Novices. They quickly abandoned that idea and briefly leased the building to the Washington Literary Institute, a private school for boys. When the Jesuits noticed that the many distractions in Georgetown City were interfering with the training of its young seminarians, it evicted the Literary Institute and opened a House of Philosophy in the building for Jesuit Scholastics, chartered under the auspices of Georgetown College. To make the enterprise self-supporting, they started a day school for lay students using the Seminary's theology and philosophy students as faculty. The school was an immediate success, enrolling children from the best Catholic and non-Catholic families in Washington City.

From the beginning, the Seminary ran afoul of its own clerical restrictions. In the early 1800s, the regulations of the Society of Jesus forbade the collection of tuition. Interestingly, Georgetown College itself was exempt from this rule. For several years, a unique money-laundering scheme existed between St. Patrick's and the local Jesuits whereby the church pastor collected the Seminary tuition while paying the Jesuits to teach.[50] Ultimately, however, orthodoxy prevailed, and the Jesuit teachers were forced to depart the school in 1827. St. Patrick's continued educating young men in a smaller school, first in the old U.S. Capitol (used for the Congress while the original Capitol building was being repaired after the War of 1812) and then back at the Washington Seminary Building, until the tuition restrictions were suspended and the Jesuits returned in 1848. As the enrollment of the Washington Seminary grew, its ties to Georgetown College diminished. It received its own charter, signed by President Buchanan in 1858, as Gonzaga College, named for St. Aloysius Gonzaga, a sixteenth-century Jesuit saint.[51]

In 1871, as the F Street neighborhood transformed from a simple village to a bustling commercial area, Gonzaga College moved into an unused orphanage on I Street, between North Capitol Street and First Street, NW. This building, still standing and visible from Georgetown's McDonough Hall podium, is around the corner from St. Aloysius Church, consecrated by the Jesuits in 1859. When Gonzaga left the old Washington Seminary, the College leased the building to Georgetown Law School, which would remain there for ten years. Gonzaga College struggled and flourished several times during the next hundred years, serving the Irish boys who moved into Swampoodle after the Civil War. It still occupies the old orphanage building, as well as several other buildings on I Street, and is still authorized to grant degrees in the Arts and Sciences, although the higher education program has long been abandoned. Today it is known as

Gonzaga High School and is one of the premier private high schools in the region. Moreover, it is remembered as a pioneer in our neighborhood.

The corner parcel of the original Washington Seminary land was sold by Gonzaga to the Freemasons in 1865. Their Grand Lodge was built by Joseph W. von Kammerhueber[52] and Adolf Cluss,[53] the dominant architect in Washington from the mid-1860s until his retirement in 1890. The Masonic Hall, built in the Italian Renaissance style, was the first large building erected in Washington after the Civil War. Completed as a mixed-use building in 1868, Cluss used polychrome stone and cast-iron veneers on the brick walls, making it then and now one of the more interesting facades in the City. At one time, it was a most sought-after ball venue for debutantes, dignitaries, and visiting royalty. Gonzaga commencements were also held there for some time. The Masons abandoned the Hall for larger quarters in 1908,[54] but the building stands today, still an architectural gem but faded from its former glory. True to its mixed-use heritage, the first floor now houses McCormick and Schmick's Restaurant. Gonzaga, straddled with huge debt, sold the rest of the Seminary property at 9th and F Streets, NW, in 1882 and Georgetown Law School, still financially shaky but poised for expansion, was forced to move to another site.

The old Washington Seminary was demolished and replaced by a block of several commercial buildings.[55] Those too were torn down some thirty years later when the Gallaudet family sold the land.[56] Two banks were subsequently built on the Seminary site adjacent to the Masonic Hall. The Equitable Bank, chartered in 1879 as the Equitable Cooperative Building Association, was one of the city's oldest and most successful savings and loans before it moved to Maryland in 1970. Its building, designed in 1911 by Frederick Pyle and Arthur Heaton,[57] has, as described in the National Register of Historic Buildings, colossal white marble Ionic columns and an interior banking hall modeled on a Greek Temple plan. It is an extraordinary example of Classical Revival Bank architecture. The old bank now houses the nightclub Platinum, and carries the 915 F Street address of the old Washington Seminary and the Law School. The adjacent Columbia National Bank, also on the Seminary site at 911 F Street, houses another nightclub called Home. I am told that many Georgetown undergraduate and law students are familiar with both clubs. I wonder if they know that they are dancing on a part of Georgetown Law Center history.

XI

TOPPING OFF

APRIL 4, 2003

The warm spring weather has allowed us to quicken the pace of our many tasks. On some days, over one hundred men and women are working on the site. We have begun to remove the yellow post shores from the lower levels of Hotung, a signal that the concrete floors have cured long enough to support themselves. The interior work has begun, as the block walls on the parking level begin to take form. Backfill operations should be concluded by the end of next week, sealing from view, perhaps forever, the various strata of subsurface soil, rock, and sand. The lap pool has now been framed and the drainage system is set and buried. Next week, the shotcrete[58] will be powered into place and the pool will become visible. The two townhouses south of Gewirz have been demolished, setting in motion dreams for future buildings.

As the steel frame of the Sport and Fitness Center continues to rise, we reach a major milestone in our construction. In the construction trades, topping off a building signifies that it has reached its ultimate height. On Monday, April 7, the final sections of concrete roofing will be poured and we will top off the Hotung Building. Although the penthouses for heating, ventilating, and air conditioning (HVAC), and other utilities have yet to be built on the roof, the infrastructure of the Hotung International Law Building will be complete. You will then look upon its final height. Whiting-Turner crews will celebrate this event with a special lunch, a simple ceremony in comparison to some celebrations in the past.

Topping-off ceremonies have existed for centuries and take many forms. The roots of these ceremonies are steeped in magic. They conjure up the blessings of the gods as well as survival of the mortals. Their origins may be lost in time, but writers for magazines such as *Modern Steel Construction* and *The Ironworker* speculate on their foundations, and I borrow from them for this note.[59] We know that when the Romans completed the Pons Sublicus across the Tiber River in 621 B.C., they threw people into the river as a sacrifice to the water gods for disturbing its flow. The ancient Chinese, perhaps more solicitous of their workers, tried to trick their gods into sending good joss by smearing chicken blood as a substitute for the human life force on the ridge poles of new structures. Some

The Hotung Building topped off
WHITING TURNER CONSTRUCTION PHOTO; BOB CREAMER, PHOTOGRAPHER

gods were fooled while others, perhaps those of the wind and fire, angrily destroyed the buildings and their scheming crews. When the river gods destroyed a bridge built by Xerxes, the monarch ordered the river, and thus the gods, to be punished with 3,000 lashes of a whip.

Because of the relationship between building materials, nature gods, and human habitats, trees were often part of ancient topping-off ceremonies. The first known ceremony to use plant branches to top off a structure occurred in Egypt's Third Dynasty (2700 B.C.) when the slaves of King Zoer placed a live plant on the top of the first stone pyramid built at Sakkara. In doing so, they hoped to ensure that the eternal life secured for Zoer by his tomb would be shared by the slaves who built it. By 700 A.D., Scandinavians were placing evergreens on ridge poles to signal the start of construction, while Teutonic tribes used them to signal completion. The practice also became prominent in the ceremonies celebrating the completion of Gothic Cathedrals, and then spread throughout France, Spain, Italy, and England during the Renaissance. Saplings, flowers, and sheaves of corn continue to adorn European homes to bring good luck to their owners. Even the practical and cosmopolitan Swiss lay a claim to the fir tree as a topping-off symbol.

Although the late nineteenth-century European immigration brought many of these traditions to the emerging industrial America, Native Americans also lay claim to the tree tradition in topping-off ceremonies. Some believe the people of the Mohawk Nation brought it to the American steel industry. The Mohawk men, seemingly immune to the vertigo of heights, performed much of the steel construction on New York skyscrapers. According to some stories, the Indians believed man-made structures should never be taller than the trees. In symbolic appeasement for this breach of the natural order, or to trick the gods like the Chinese of old, they brought a tree to the top of a building when it reached its structural summit. Notwithstanding the importance of the tree, most early twentieth-century photos show an American flag rather than a tree in the topping off ceremonies of that era. The flag joined or replaced the tree when steel workers began using it as a patriotic protest against the so-called "American Plan," launched in 1919 to destroy the union movement.[60] We expect the American flag to have a prominent place in our ceremony.

Ceremonies to appease the gods have always existed. Perhaps to evoke our own primal memory, many continue in some form today. Indian corn adorns our homes at Thanksgiving and mistletoe and trees complement our Christmases, each harkening back to ceremonies that at one time appeased and celebrated the nature gods. Houses are often blessed by holy men and some are built according to the Eastern principles of feng shui.[61] Indeed, in recognition of Mr. Hotung's ancestry, we consulted feng shui designers to ensure that his gift to the Law Center would be consistent with the principles of energy or "life breath"[62] associated with this tradition. Abe Pollin,[63] a friend of the Law Center, gave us a coin to toss into our concrete foundations, a ritual he performs in all of his buildings and one we continued in ours.

American labor issues and the gods of old have both evolved, but trees and flags continue to be part of many American topping-off celebrations. Our celebration will be much more simple than those of the past, but our wish for good joss and our thankfulness for the absence of fatal injuries on our project will be just as real.[64]

The steel frame of the Sport and Fitness Center
WHITING TURNER CONSTRUCTION PHOTO; BOB CREAMER, PHOTOGRAPHER

XII

STEEL

APRIL 28, 2003

It is a rare treat to watch two buildings with different structural frames go up side by side. With the completion of the concrete work in the Hotung Building, the yellow deck supports are being removed and the internal work begins in earnest. The swimming pool pan is in place and the pool deck will soon be poured. Ducts are being installed to carry heated and cooled air throughout the building and the boilers and chillers have actually been delivered. Conduit for the electrical wire and pipe for the plumbing are also being connected. Stairways are being installed, interior walls are being built in the lower levels, and the back-up cinder-block for the facing brick is being set.

Steel columns and beams form the structure of the Sport and Fitness Center. (See photo on page 38.) The third- and fourth-floor metal decks that will support the concrete floor are being installed and the columns to the roof are being erected. After the beams are lifted into place by heavy cranes, iron workers walk the beams to weld or torque the pieces together, just as they did a century ago. In case you have been wondering, the beams connecting the Sport and Fitness Center to Gewirz are correctly set at an angle. The roof at this section will drain to the east. When the building is completed, the parapet on the front at this section will extend above the roof, thus hiding the sloping condition. The same engineering will occur where Sport and Fitness connects to the Hotung Building.

The importance of iron and steel to the modern world cannot be denied. For this section, the "steel" entry of the *Encyclopedia Britannica* provided much of the information.[65] Iron production, the forerunner of steel production, began in Anatolia about 2000 B.C. and spread widely throughout the inhabited world. By 1000 B.C., the Iron Age was well established. The technology for iron production reached into western Europe by 500 B.C., and by 400 B.C. it had reached China. Africa also lays claim to early iron production.

The ancients were not able to produce liquid iron because their furnaces were not capable of reaching the high temperatures necessary to do so. According to the *Encyclopedia Britannica*, "early iron was produced in small shaft furnaces as [soft but] solid lumps of iron oxide, slag and charcoal, called blooms. The blooms were then hot forged into bars of wrought iron, a malleable material containing bits of slag and charcoal. The carbon contents of the early irons ranged from very low (0.07 percent) to high (0.8 percent), the latter constituting a genuine steel."

Iron was so highly prized in Egypt that a small iron dagger was buried with King Tut in 1343 B.C. The Egyptians improved their production process by 900 B.C., and were able to temper their steel to reduce its brittleness. They and others used it to produce a material that was ideally suited to the fabrication of swords and knives. There is also some evidence that the Chinese could produce heat-treated steel during the early Han dynasty (206 B.C.– 25 A.D.). These early smiths probably didn't understand the importance of carbon in the production of steel. They did know, however, that if they heated their iron over charcoal fires and prayed or uttered magic incantations, sturdy weapons would result. Those prayers and incantations may have measured the proper time to heat the iron to absorb the carbon from the charcoal. Whatever their theory, the ancient smiths were able to make fire-tempered weapons that were far superior to the bronze weapons of their enemies. The Romans, prodigious users of such weaponry, helped to spread the knowledge of iron-making; but after their decline, centuries passed without significant improvements to the production of steel.

Iron, and its derivative, steel, are not easy to produce without high temperatures and controlled heat. Although ancient civilizations were able to extract iron from its ore and create fine weapons, the process was largely misunderstood until modern times. In the fifteenth century, smiths began to use waterpower with large bellows to blow air into the furnaces, thereby increasing the temperature within. The increased heat reduced the metal to a liquid rich in carbon. The liquid iron was much easier to shape than the solid iron blooms. The technology continued to improve for the next few hundred years, permitting ever-increasing temperatures to be attained in the furnaces. The large open-hearth furnace was developed by William and Friedrich Siemens in 1860, achieving temperatures of 3,600 degrees Fahrenheit, and a load capacity of 300 tons of steel. In 1855, Henry Bessemer developed a process that would boost steel mill productivity more than any other single development in the twentieth century, and ultimately lead to the replacement of most of the open hearths with basic oxygen furnaces. In 1907, Bethlehem Steel installed a mill capable of processing giant forty-eight-inch-wide flange beams. These beams, which allowed builders to employ longer spans and design simpler columns, led to a renewed interest in skyscraper and steel bridge construction at the turn of the century. Structural steel remained the primary material for skyscrapers until the 1960s when designers began to use steel/concrete composite frames.

The *Encyclopedia Britannica* defines steel as "a hard, strong, durable, and malleable alloy of iron and carbon, in which the carbon content ranges up to 2 percent." It often contains other constituents such as manganese, chromium, nickel, molybdenum, copper, tungsten, cobalt, or silicon, depending on the desired alloy properties. It is the most widely used material for building the world's infrastructure. With it, one can make everything, from pins to skyscrapers and from toasters to aircraft carriers. Moreover, the tools required to fabricate these items are made from the same alloys, suggesting a magic similar to that relied on by the early fabricators. Our need for steel seems virtually limitless. The world's steel production a few years ago "was about 795 million tons, while production of the next most important engineering metal, aluminum, was only about 21 million tons. The main reasons for the popularity of steel [over other metals] are its relatively low fabrication, forming, and processing costs, the abundance of its two raw materials (iron ore and scrap), and its unparalleled range of mechanical properties," according to the *Encyclopedia Britannica.*

The modern history of steel is the history of the industrial revolution itself. The names Krupp and Siemens, Carnegie, Morgan, and Weir conjure visions of the massive, fiery, open-hearth furnaces of Pittsburgh, Germany, and England, of the unimaginable wealth of the steel barons, and of the dangerous and dependent lives of iron and steel workers. Today, steel production is cleaner, safer, and leaner, and remains on the edge of modern technology. Mini-mills are rapidly replacing the behemoths of the past. Electric arc furnaces now produce steel, but still operate alongside the basic oxygen furnace and the ever dwindling number of open hearths. New alloys yield strengths greater than conventional steel. The technology improves so rapidly that half of today's steel grades didn't exist ten years ago. Once on the site, however, the technology recedes and the steel walkers connect beam to column, performing their timeless industrial dance against the skyline.

The Cairo Apartment Building, designed in the Egyptian Revival Style, is responsible for height limits in Washington, D.C. LIBRARY OF CONGRESS, PRINTS AND PHOTOGRAPHS DIVISION

XIII

CONCRETE TOWNS AND STEEL TOWNS

MAY 13, 2003

Barring unforeseen delays, the tower crane will be dismantled at the end of this week. This powerful work-horse of our project has become a familiar and friendly vision to many of us. Before the buildings rose, it was the symbol of the things to come. Now, its job is finished and we move on to other tasks. Its departure signals the end of major concrete work and reminds us how close we are to completing this project. If we stay on schedule, we will be finished in just over one year.

The current work on Hotung is essential, but not enticing to the eye. The last remaining post shores are being removed, the backfill on the south side is nearly complete, and the backing brick called concrete masonry units (CMU) are slowly rising up the Hotung facade. On our visits to the top floors, we now use a recently completed stairway rather than the rickety construction stairway we used before.

At the Sport and Fitness Center, however, the dramatic dangling steel beams continue to draw our attention. The largest trusses will be mounted this week and next. The bowed front of the Sport and Fitness Center, rising up the second and third floor facade, is now visible. Its design complements the slight bow in the Hotung north end and the cylindrical drum-shaped entrances of our other buildings. At the fourth floor, the Sport and Fitness facade steps back, providing an accessible mezzanine that will overlook the F Street Green. Inside the bow, in a two-story atrium, students will study and relax in a lounge area that will open to a terrace on the green.

The concrete work winds down, but it is not quite complete. As steel continues to rise, we are pumping concrete onto the metal decks of the Sport and Fitness Center. The relationship between concrete and steel is an interesting one. In the construction trades, America cities are considered either concrete towns or steel towns, depending on the building material typically used to create their skylines. Baltimore, for example, is a steel town. Washington, on the other hand, is a concrete town. As you might imagine, the cost and availability of material and local labor are the biggest drivers of the concrete/steel decision. Structural depth also plays a role, especially in D.C.

Concrete, you may remember, is made from inexpensive sand and rocks that are found almost everywhere; steel, however, is expensive to fabricate relative to concrete and often has a volatile pricing structure. Large numbers of concrete workers are needed to build the forms, bundle the reinforcing steel, and guide the pour. Steel requires fewer workers to rivet or weld the beams. Moreover, steel structures take far less time to erect. You can see, for example, how quickly the steel structural frame of the Sport and Fitness Center is going up compared to the time it took to erect the concrete structure of Hotung.

In every construction project, contractors and owners balance design elements with these variable costs to determine which type of building will be more cost-effective. Still other factors may make a pure cost calculation incomplete. For example, the height limitation imposed on buildings in the District of Columbia is the major reason why Washington is a concrete town. When the Territory of Columbia was created, both Jefferson and Washington favored height limitations. Jefferson's experience in Paris convinced him that buildings should be "low and convenient, and the streets light and airy."[66] George Washington also wanted to preserve clear views of the heroic public buildings he planned to commission in Washington City, but he also had more practical concerns. He worried about structural and fire safety in addition to aesthetic delights.[67] The concerns of both men easily found their way into Pierre L'Enfant's original "grand plan."

Although many people think that either the Washington Monument or the Capitol Dome is the reference point for D.C.'s height limitation, the Cairo Apartments, built in 1894 at 1615 Q Street, NW, was the cause of the statutory limitation. The design of the Cairo is a mere architectural curiosity today, but it sparked an aesthetic outrage among architects and civic leaders at the turn of the century. Then, as now, it was the tallest apartment building in Washington, D.C., visibly taller if one takes the time to study it. Towering high above its neighboring churches and residences, (See photo on page 42.) the Cairo was viewed as "arrogant" by the citizens of that day. Its Egyptian Revival facade, derived from buildings at the 1890 Chicago Exposition, did nothing to lessen the anger of its critics. In response to this civic outrage, Congress passed legislation, still in effect today, that limits the height of buildings to 160 feet, the height of the Cairo.[68] For over one hundred years, this height limitation has preserved the horizontal nature of Washington that Pierre L'Enfant originally envisioned. It is why the soaring skyscrapers of Chicago and New York are absent from our skyline and why, ultimately, D.C. remains a concrete town.

When the cost of construction is calculated in D.C., the more floors one can construct in a building's height, the more quickly one will recover an investment and increase the project's profit. Because concrete permits a significantly shallower depth between floors and ceilings than does steel, concrete buildings can have more stories and thus, more usable space than steel buildings of the same height. Our two buildings, for example, are essentially the same height and yet Hotung has one more story than the Sport and Fitness Center (well, actually two more in function since the basketball gym is double height).

Given the fact that both of our buildings are well below the city's height limitation, one must wonder why Hotung is built with concrete while steel forms the structural frame of the Sport and Fitness Building. Hotung was built of concrete for both space and cost reasons. We wanted to maximize the amount of usable space we could build within our budget. We could not use the same formula when planning the Sport and Fitness Center, however, because of constructability issues. You may recall that the reinforcing steel rods within concrete increase its tensile strength. Nonetheless, there are limits. Even reinforced steel and elegant arches cannot easily span very large spaces. Concrete beams will eventually collapse of their own weight as the distance between columns gets larger. Even where spanning long distances with concrete is technically possible, it is often economically impractical. Thus, steel is typically used for long spans. There are some exceptions to this formula. The ribbed thin-shell concrete structure of the former Seattle Kingdome and the precast post-tensioned concrete structure of the Sydney Opera House are notable examples.

The Sport and Fitness Center has two large spans, one over the lap pool and one over the basketball court. Only steel can economically connect its columns and support the weight above these large spans. The beams covering these two spans are substantial. Those running north and south across the pool weigh 6,000 pounds each. The major trusses, soon to be set in place above the basketball court, extend for over one hundred feet and weigh 22,000 pounds each. To gain the same strength from concrete, one might need ten to twelve times that weight to support the same load. Thus, our buildings are constructed differently for specific reasons, although they will be complementary in external design.

In an earlier chapter, I wrote about the remarkable range of products made from steel. My "pins to skyscrapers" statement prompted a reader of the original "Construction Notes" to tell me that the Bessemer process not only rejuvenated interest in skyscrapers, but also revolutionized women's fashion. She relates that into the late 1850s, women's bell-shaped skirts were supported by crinoline petticoats that were stiffened by whalebone/baleen. Due to the size of whalebone/baleen, the largest skirts could be only four feet in diameter. Bessemer's innovation allowed for the low-cost production of flexible steel bands or strapping. The steel bands were then turned into hoops held together by cloth tapes, which then supported the famous huge hoop skirts of the Civil War era. Some of these hoop skirts were over eight feet wide, producing fodder for cartoonists of the day. Bessemer's process permitted the skirts to be sold at a cost that was affordable for the general public.

I also wrote earlier that the steel industry was becoming leaner and that the behemoth furnaces of the past were being replaced by mini-mills. Bethlehem Steel, giant of the industry, creator of the flange beam, and producer of the steel that built the Golden Gate Bridge, closed its doors at the end of April, 2003.[69]

The Lenman Building (arrow), Georgetown Law Center's third home flanked by the NS&T Building
GEORGETOWN LAW CENTER ARCHIVE

XIV

THE LAW CENTER'S THIRD AND FOURTH HOMES

JUNE 17, 2003

The first few weeks of summer break have brought both progress and delay to the Campus Completion Project. Because the steel walkers are not tethered when they set steel and weld or rivet it together, the many long days of rain have delayed the rising of the Sport and Fitness Center's steel frame.[70] Nonetheless, the dramatic tree-branch front columns are almost completely set and the columns and beams up to the cardio/aerobic level have been fireproofed. The fourth-floor concrete slab is in place, the metal deck for the mezzanine mechanical room awaits a concrete slab, and the decking for the roof begins this week. The wall separating Gewirz and the Sport and Fitness Center at the parking level has been breached, connecting all three buildings for the first time.

The details of the Hotung Building are becoming more visible. The steel for the floating library staircases on the second and third floors have been set. The views from the third-floor stairway, overlooking the F Street Green, will be inspiring. The yellow and blue air barrier is being applied and the precast sills for the windows are being installed to the lower levels of the east side of Hotung, all in anticipation of the windows and the facing brick. Inside, CMU walls are going up, and air ducts, wiring, and plumbing continue to be installed. And, if you have not noticed, the generator is finally gone, only six months later than Potomac Electric Power Company (PEPCO) had promised.

Several months ago, I related the history of the Law Center's second home in the old Washington Seminary/Gonzaga building at 915 F Street, NW. When Gonzaga moved to North Capitol and I Streets, NE, and consolidated its operations, the Jesuits sold the seminary property to help relieve their debt. The sale and subsequent demolition of the Seminary building forced the Law School to seek another home. Georgetown's third and fourth homes occupied buildings that were sturdy, if somewhat common, examples of nineteenth-century urban architecture. In 1882, the Law School moved to the Lenman Building at 1425 New York Avenue, NW, near the U.S. Treasury Building. The photograph (page 46) shows a rather tall mixed-use building with an Italianate cornice typical of that era. More interesting, however, is the building next to it on the corner, which eventually expanded to replace the building thought to be the Lenman. The National Safe Deposit Company and National Savings Bank, forebears of the National Savings and Trust Bank, occupied the site at the corner of 15th Street and New York Avenue, NW, across from the Treasury Building, since at least 1856.[71] In 1888, they demolished the building and erected a new bank in the eclectic commercial style of the late nineteenth century. If one looks at the NS & T building today, the structure appears to be one large red brick building stretching halfway down New York Avenue. In fact, it was erected in three separate stages. First in 1916, and then in 1925, NS & T expanded its original 1888 building, matching brick, stone, and style with such precision that the additions are hardly noticeable. Even the passage of time has not diminished the work of their master bricklayers.

The building in our photograph that purports to be the Lenman building would have been demolished for the 1925 addition. By then, Georgetown was long gone. I have some doubt, however, that the building portrayed in our photograph is the Lenman Building. Lenman owned several properties on the block but none had the 1425 address. Plats from that time show the addresses going from 1423 to 1427, with no 1425. Addresses of that time, however, do not always correspond to present-day numbering. The property shown in the photograph is more likely to be 1421 or 1419 New York Avenue, not 1425. Today, 1425 New York Avenue is an office building, erected in the 1980s, that houses parts of the Department of Justice.

Although the Lenman building may have held little architectural distinction, Georgetown's brief stay there marked the beginning of its journey to academic prominence. In the 1882 term, Georgetown had an enrollment of forty-six students who each paid $80 per year for tuition, and who received an LL.B. degree after two years of study.[72] In 1881, the D.C. Bar passed a rule that required three years of legal education for admission to the Bar. In response, Georgetown began offering a one-year Master of Laws program. Master's degree candidates paid $40 per year for tuition. Because of a thriving economy, its proximity to the courts, and a faculty that included many judges and an occasional Supreme Court Justice, law school enrollments began to grow. By 1890, a mere eight years after the move to the Lenman Building, enrollment exceeded 250.[73] Thus, the Law School had achieved financial and academic security for the first time since its birth. This rapid expansion prompted a writer in the November 1883 *Georgetown College Journal* to say, "It is no longer a matter of doubt that the Law School of Georgetown is destined to stand head and shoulders above the dozens or more similar institutions of which the National Capital can boast."[74]

The increase in enrollments quickly rendered the Lenman building too small to conduct classes. In 1884, Georgetown was forced to move again, this time to the southeast corner of 6th and F Streets, NW.[75] The move east to the boundary between the old downtown and the old East End again brought the Law School close to the courts and the center of commercial life. The increasing revenue permitted it to rent, and contemplate purchasing, this house where the emerging F Street businesses and the remaining residential buildings that once dominated this area mingled.

The 1884 home was originally a family residence,[76] renovated to accommodate the "lecture and quiz" method of education commonly used in law schools of the era. The renovation was apparently successful. As the students and faculty moved in, the *Georgetown College Journal* reported that "the taste displayed and the comfortableness attained in all the appointments of the lecture rooms passed the [high] calculations of everyone."[77] The photo (page 50) of the building shows design features from many architectural styles. Because of its mansard roof, however, it is considered to be of the Second Empire style.[78] During the 1860s and 1870s, American architects borrowed the double-pitched roof with its steep lower slope and other features of Second Empire style from France and made them popular in Washington City. The Renwick Gallery, located less than a block from the White House on Pennsylvania Avenue and completed in 1861, is an elegant and more precise example of Second Empire architecture than is the law school building. Georgetown's building was not a pure Second Empire style building. It incorporated values of Federal, Italianate, Neoclassical, and Queen Anne architectural styles in addition to the distinctive mansard roof. The mid-1800s was an architectural era of "picturesque eclecticism," during which designers freely combined elements of several different styles. Today, the old "picturesque eclecticism" of the house on the site has given way to ghastly governmental modernism. Engine Company Number 2 of the D.C. Fire Department now resides in a dreary bunker on the southeast corner of 6th and F Streets.

Georgetown's residential neighbors of the era were both illustrious and notorious. Mary Surratt, a conspirator in the Lincoln assassination who was hanged (perhaps unjustly) for her involvement, ran a boardinghouse at 604 H Street, NW, before her death.[79] Her house is still standing. Supreme Court Justice Salmon Chase, and then his daughter Kate and her husband, Senator William Sprague lived at 6th and E Streets, NW, (a site now occupied by the AARP) until their divorce. South of Pennsylvania Avenue, however, the residents were more bawdy. On a site near today's National Museum of the American Indian, Mary Ann Hall ran the most exclusive and expensive of Washington's brothels.[80] Perhaps the most interesting resident for Georgetown's purposes was two-time presidential candidate Belva Ann Lockwood, who lived at 619 F Street for forty years.[81] Ms. Lockwood was also the first woman admitted to the Supreme Court. She gained admittance after Congress passed her bill permitting women to practice before all the courts of the United States. Earlier in her life, Georgetown had refused to admit her to the Law School because she was a woman. She went on to study at the National Law School and then at the Columbian Law School, which ultimately became George Washington.[82] Georgetown would not change its policies regarding women students until the early 1950s.

The years between 1884 and 1891 were prosperous ones for Georgetown. Thus, the Law School's $600 rent, which was rather steep for the time, was easily payable even in its first year of residence. During the seven years that the Law School occupied the building at 6th and F Streets, enrollment increased yearly, growing to 253 in 1890.[83] The prestige of the school increased as well, prompting one writer to say that Georgetown was "recognized as one of the foremost schools of instruction in all essential branches of the law in the United States ...and that its diploma had come to be recognized as a sure passport in all professional circles in every state in the Federal Union."[84] Although this building was once thought to be a final home, the Law School's academic and financial success led to yet another home, one that would be built and owned by Georgetown in 1891, and one destined to be its home for the next eighty years.

The townhouse at 6th and F Streets, NW, Georgetown Law Center's fourth home
GEORGETOWN LAW CENTER ARCHIVE

XV

THINGS YOU WILL NEVER SEE

JULY 31, 2003

Despite delays caused by our rainy summer, our project remains essentially on schedule. The roof deck has been completed in the Sport and Fitness Center, and we have topped off the building. The yellow and blue air barrier continues to be applied to the Hotung Building, and precast sills and face brick are being set on the first floor of the east elevation. As the brick goes up, one can begin to visualize the look of the building's exterior. Metal studs frame the walls on several floors inside the Hotung Building, offering a visual sense of the interior room layouts as well.

CMU continues to be laid at the Hotung penthouse and inside both buildings. Glazed interior block has been laid in the pool area of the Sport and Fitness Center providing the first sense of inside color. All of the steel beams and columns in the Sport and Fitness Center, except those associated with the roof, have been fireproofed. Pipes, ducts, and wires, all the things you will never see once the buildings are completed, are being run throughout the project.

When most people consider great architecture, both their minds and eyes are usually drawn to a building's facade. It is what we see first and, if the building is pleasing, we look at it again and again, noticing features we had not noticed before. Beautifully designed buildings enhance the experiences of our daily lives. They inspire, they delight. They enliven neighborhoods, lift people's spirits, and occasionally become part of the cultural vernacular of cities and nations.[85]

Once beyond the front doors, eyes and minds again consider appearance, this time of the interiors. Soon, however, thoughts of beauty recede and people begin to consider how a building works. If the public spaces permit an easy flow of patrons, if people work in offices that are adjacent to colleagues whose work complements theirs, and if natural light enhances the work space that one inhabits, the building is deemed comfortable, the work produced in it will be performed efficiently, and the residents will be satisfied. When efficiency combines with gracious style, the building adds to the grand architectural spaces of great cities.

Of course, beautiful buildings do not always work. Office buildings today are sometimes deemed sick, so environmentally contaminated that work cannot be performed within them. The beauty of those buildings is soon ignored as the occupants begin to fall ill. Occupants of a Richmond, Virginia office building kept getting mysterious insect bites until a missing set of filters were installed. Loose particles of fiberglass had been blowing through the ventilation system onto employees' skin and causing the mysterious bites.[86] Structural defects may also occur, as when the windows fell to the street some years ago at the Hancock Building in Boston.[87] In some cases, floors or beams collapse, even before the building is occupied. A combination of unexpected wind and incomplete welding brought down beams during the construction of the new D.C. Convention Center.[88] Mechanical systems may prove to be insufficient, electrical circuits too small, plumbing ineffective. Many mechanical problems were discovered in our McDonough Building after it was erected. We have been correcting them ever since.

What permits us to concentrate on the splendor of a beautiful building is not only its design and the absence of major flaws, but also the continuous operation of all the things we never see — the wires, the conduit, the pipes, the ducts — all hidden in the walls and floors and even under the ground, all of which are taken for granted as we use a building daily, all of which must be designed perfectly and unobtrusively if our eye is to continue to be drawn to the beauty of our building.

Approximately 35% of the cost of a building goes to MEP — mechanical, electrical, and plumbing systems. Much of the equipment covered by these costs will be placed in one of the nine mechanical rooms located in the lower levels or on the roofs of the Hotung Building and the Sport and Fitness Center. Heating and cooling plants, air handling equipment to distribute hot and/or cold air, and water pumps to distribute hot and/or cold water for air conditioning, toilets, sinks, and water-coolers all share these mechanical rooms. Other pumps, such as those that distribute water to standpipes for fire hoses, to ceiling sprinklers, and to the swimming pool purification systems, are also found there.

Water literally surrounds a building. Engineers weave intricate plumbing patterns that bring needed water into a building while ensuring that unwanted water moves out or is kept out. Waste water flows out of the building though cast-iron pipes into the city's sewers, and finally to treatment plants, while storm water collected on the buildings' roofs must be diverted away from that treatment system to storm drains and sand filters. Drain tiles collect water running down the building's facade and direct it to other filters and storm drains. Foundations are waterproofed so that ground water, or in our case, an emerging trickle from the old Tiber Creek, does not intrude to weaken our foundation or produce mold. Fifteen thousand feet of copper tubing will bring water into our buildings and 8,000 feet of cast iron pipe winds through the buildings to remove it.

In modern buildings, we turn night into daylight with the flip of a switch. For this magic to occur, electrical wires move from ten-foot-deep vaults under the street, through duct banks into a building, and then through a conduit to those switches. They provide temporary power for the cranes and other construction needs, and then eventually illuminate and power the finished buildings. Hundreds of circuit breakers check overloads and prevent electrical fires. Moreover, no matter what the size of the room, the light always seems appropriate for the surroundings. All this is made possible by the 45,000 feet of conduit and the forty-three miles of electrical wiring that course through the buildings.

Again in modern buildings, we breathe easily, never too warm, never too cold, as we go about our business. 6,000 feet of steel pipe moves the water throughout our buildings for heating and cooling. Chillers and boilers cool or heat the air, remove the excess moisture, and move the air noiselessly through the building to keep us comfortable. Pumps remove and recycle the old air so we do not become ill or die. Our chillers provide seven hundred tons of capacity for cooling. A normal household unit provides three tons. The boilers for both buildings produce 8,280,000 BTUs for heating. A household unit averages about 92,000 BTUs.[89]

One of the more intriguing elements of the things we do not see once a building is completed is now visible. Most of the east side of the Hotung Building is covered with blue and yellow materials. The blue material, called "Blue Skin," is a rubberized-asphalt barrier that comes in self-adhering sheets. The yellow material is a product called Air-Block 21S. It is a synthetic rubber-based insulating adhesive, diluted with a solvent and sprayed on. These materials act as vapor barrier, air barrier, and damp-proofing for the building. Vapor barriers control the flow of humidity through a wall. When warmer air hits cooler temperatures, the moisture in the air can condense into water somewhere within the wall. The water can then cause mold growth, rot, or in freezing temperatures, ice, which can rip a wall apart little by little. Based on a building's inside design temperatures, on historic outside temperatures of the locality, and on the insulating values of all the wall components, engineers and architects can calculate the dew point and predict where condensation will occur. Vapor barriers are placed on the warm side of the dew point to slow the flow of moisture from the warmer moist air to the colder air where moisture might condense. In predominantly cold climates the vapor barrier goes on the inside. In predominantly warm climates it goes on the outside. In D.C., vapor barriers are placed on the outside.

Air barriers prevent the flow of air through a wall. Air flowing through a wall will decrease the energy efficiency of a building. In addition, as warm air moves to colder areas, condensation can accumulate in the form of puddles of water on a floor in the summer or large dangerous icicles in the winter. Both will be avoided if the air barrier is installed and is effective. Any solid material devoid of cracks or holes can be used as an air barrier. In our case, it is the polyethylene.

Damp-proofing requires a light-duty material designed to prevent water that makes incidental contact with a wall from penetrating a building. As gravity moves rain water down the face brick, the damp-proofing prevents water from seeping through the wall.

In a climate like D.C.'s, which is equally warm and cold, a single material is used as the vapor barrier, air barrier, and damp-proofing. This material is placed between the CMU wall, where you see it now, and the insulating material that will soon fill the brick cavity. The insulating material, two inches of rigid extruded polystyrene, is the same material used in Styrofoam cups. It will be placed between the face brick and the CMU wall. If condensation develops, it will occur in the insulated area and be weeped out through the brick cavity.

None of these processes are left to chance. Engineers spend days calculating air volume, square footage, intended use, geographical climate, historic rainwater levels, shading coefficients, and ratios of glass to solid wall. Once they are all calculated, the requirements are increased beyond recommended standards to ensure that the building operates efficiently and consistently. Our project is especially complex because two very different buildings, containing multiple and normally non-compatible functions, are being engineered as essentially one structure. Libraries, food service, classrooms, swimming pools, and gyms all have different engineering needs. Yet all will work together when construction is completed.

The buildings we are erecting promise to be pleasing to the eye as well as efficient and comfortable. They will enhance our neighborhood and the experiences of the Georgetown community. They are beautifully designed and engineered, with elegant systems hidden behind the walls, a system of calculated complexity that you will never see.

The Law Center's first owned property, designed by James F. Denson
GEORGETOWN LAW CENTER ARCHIVE

XVI

THE E STREET WAREHOUSE

SEPTEMBER 9, 2003

Although the seemingly endless rains of summer delayed steel placement and masonry work on the Hotung International Building and the Sport and Fitness Center, we made significant progress not only on the new buildings but also on renovations to McDonough Hall and to the Gewirz Residence Center. The dazzling new cafeteria in McDonough is a feat of architectural legerdemain. Not only have we transformed a pedestrian and inefficient food venue into a veritable work of art, we did so in one-third of the time ordinarily expected for such a project. In Gewirz, we turned our outdated Public Safety command post into a high-tech security communication center, without compromising the architectural integrity of the Office of Residence Life. Last week, reconstruction of the Day Care Center playground began.

At the Campus Completion Project, face brick and precast concrete sills have been installed up to the sixth floor on the east side of Hotung. Scaffolding is up on the west elevation and masonry work has begun on the south side. Lintels and frames for the soaring arched windows on the east and west elevations are now in place, and the trusses for the east side cornice are being installed. CMU masonry work is almost complete on the west and south sides of Sport and Fitness, and ground face and glazed blocks are being set in various pool and exercise areas. Elevator shafts are being prepared, stairways are being completed, and door frames and metal wall studs are in place, awaiting the installation of drywall some time in early 2004. HVAC (heating, ventilation, and air conditioning) and freshwater piping continues to rise while stormwater piping and roof drains move downward. Air handling units have been assembled and sheet metal for boiler flues is being set. More than 120 workers are on the site each day, and although weather continues to pose challenges to our schedule, we are still expecting a June 2004 completion date.

As we pause to assess our summer progress, thoughts return to the Law Center's history and to the architectural achievements attained in our prior buildings. For the first twenty-one years after its founding in 1870, the law school lived a peripatetic existence, renting four buildings during that time. In

November of 1891, the Law School dedicated its fifth building, the first one that Georgetown actually owned. At the opening ceremony, Judge Martin Morris, the dean and one of the founders of the law school, noted:

> Our new building, which we occupy for the first time this evening, will satisfactorily accommodate upwards of five hundred students; and we hope to rest here for many years. And yet, in some opening twenty years from this, our successors may smile at our limited ideas when they welcome a thousand or two thousand students to the study of law.[90]

Judge Morris' words now seem prophetic as we contemplate opening two new buildings on a six-acre campus for more than 2,000 J.D. and LL.M. students. Moreover, the founders' ideas and dreams, fashioned by twenty-one years of financial struggle and teaching experience, and many more years of law practice, were far from limited. Indeed, they provided a vision for the dynamic Georgetown Law Center that we have inherited and now nurture.[91]

Georgetown originally decided to build its new school at the corner of 6th and D Streets, NW. When the university failed to acquire that property, it chose a parcel one block to the north. Ownership of Georgetown's new land at 506 E Street, NW, can be traced back to 1790 when David Burnes, an original proprietor in Washington City, held it. He subsequently passed the land on to his daughter, Marcia, at his death.[92] In 1891, the law school's new site, once rural property, was at the edge of the emerging downtown. Seventh and F Streets, NW, near two of the law school's previous homes, had become the commercial hub of the City. Nearby were the courts and the old Neoclassical City Hall (now one of the buildings in the D.C. Court system),[93] and the law offices of many prominent lawyers. Even today, older D.C. lawyers fondly remember the Fifth Streeters, lawyers who occupied offices on 5th Street between Indiana Avenue and F Street, NW, and who plied their trade in the local courts well into the twentieth century.

The architecturally innovative Pension Building at 5th and G Streets, NW, designed by Montgomery Meigs,[94] had opened just four years earlier. That building now houses the National Building Museum.[95] At 4th and D Streets, NW, stood the First Presbyterian Church, the church of Presidents Jackson, Polk, Pierce, and Cleveland. Three blocks to the south stood the Baltimore and Potomac Railroad station, where, only ten years earlier, Charles Guiteau shot and mortally wounded President Garfield.[96] Notable citizens, residing in elegant Italianate-style residences, entertained just to the south at Blagden Row on Indiana Avenue, and to the east, surrounding Judiciary Square. Stretching along 6th Street, between Pennsylvania Avenue and C Street, NW, was the fashionable National Hotel.[97]

The new Law School building, completed in 1891, was designed by James F. Denson[98] in an eclectic turn-of-the-century urban style. It was a three-story, red-brick building built at a cost of $7,020.[99] It is likely that Denson's work, like that of many architects of the time, was influenced by Henry Hobson Richardson, who gave his name to the "Richardson Romanesque" style of architecture and to the architectural firm of Shepley Bulfinch Richardson and Abbott, our current lead architects. As the photo of the building (page 54) reveals, its entrance boasted the semicircular arched windows and massive arched entrance distinctive of Romanesque architecture. This entrance arch, and its lintel inscribed with the words "Law Department," are now preserved in a wall in the Library Quad between McDonough Hall and the Williams Library. Above its Romanesque entrance, however, was a Neoclassical architrave and entablature, and above that a roofline that revealed elements of the Georgian style. American architecture of the mid-to-late-1800s is sometimes called "picturesque eclecticism."[100] Although built at the end of that period, Denson's building retains some elements of that motif.

The *Georgetown College Journal* called the building "a marvel of beauty, elegance, and convenience"[101] in December of 1891. Built for six hundred students, it contained a reading room, a "spacious" twenty-foot by thirty-five-foot library, lecture rooms "without pillars or other obstructions," a faculty room and a coat and hat room for faculty, and a "magnificent hall on the third floor capable of seating more than four hundred students."[102] "The sanitary arrangements, the heating, and the ventilation of the building [were] complete in every particular ... [with] the air renewed in the entire building every few minutes."[103] Two hundred and sixty-eight students attended that year, matriculating from thirty-seven states and paying $80 in tuition plus a $10 graduation fee. Comfortable boarding arrangements could be had for between twenty and thirty dollars. The cost of books was another $30.[104]

The growth that prompted the construction of the building at 506 E Street, however, did not abate. By 1909, over six hundred students were attending the law school and Georgetown again considered new construction. In 1911, the building expanded in the same architectural style towards 6th Street, doubling in size. Two years later, an even larger section was erected on 6th Street. This wing contained a new auditorium and, from 1919 to 1934, the Georgetown Foreign Service School. Between 1934 and 1937, the Law School acquired several adjoining properties, including the old Howard Law School on Fifth Street, and Rodman's Restaurant at Fifth and E Street, NW. Rodman's was the defendant in *Cushing v. Rodman*,[105] the case which held that restaurants serving defective food would be held to strict liability. By 1950, Georgetown had acquired much of the property between 5th and 6th and D and E Streets, NW, and the Law Center,[106] as it would become known in the late 1950s, looked forward to years of prosperity and growth.

The years between 1891 and 1960 witnessed growth in program as well as facilities. By 1921, the Law School had created a day program and hired a full-time faculty. It had also become the largest law school in America. By 1936, the library held 20,000 volumes.[107] The Moot Court, one of the first programs established at the Law School in 1870, continued to thrive. Names of the "Best Advocates" from 1929 on can be found on plaques outside the Philip Hart

Auditorium in McDonough Hall. The Debate Society, formed in 1893 and reorganized in 1906, fielded teams that were virtually unbeatable. Columbian Law School (later renamed George Washington) refused, after four successive defeats, to accept new challenges from Georgetown, charging "unfairness, prejudice, and unjust discrimination."[108] The Law Journal, and later the Student Bar Association, began to thrive.

The Law School remained at 506 E Street until 1971. The intervening years produced some of the giants in Georgetown history – George Hamilton, Hugh Fegan, Reverend Francis Lucey, Frank Dugan, Walter "Doc" Jaeger, Richard Allan Gordon, and Paul Dean.[109] But as the program and the personalities gained renown, the building began to deteriorate. By 1963, the building once called "a marvel of beauty, elegance, and convenience" was described by Dean Paul Dean as "the least adequate of any of the major law schools in the country" and a "nightmare."[110] At that time, the school consisted of the original Denson building with its addition, and four adjoining buildings used for library and faculty offices; "five other converted tenements comprised [the] dormitory facilities." The library occupied space in three separate buildings and on thirteen different floors.

By 1965, over 1,300 students were occupying a building originally designed for five hundred. Library books, now numbering over 125,000, were kept on the stairs going to the basement because shelf space was lacking.[111] The old downtown was deteriorating as people left the city for homes and shopping centers in the suburbs, especially after the insurrection following the assassination of Martin Luther King in 1968.[112] The dormitories were closed because they failed to meet minimum standards. Program growth and faculty expansion were stymied because there was just no space. The exterior architecture was considered passe and industrial, and the interiors had not changed in thirty-five years.

A new breed of students was coming to the Law School during the final years of the Denson building. They were impatient with the status quo, politically attuned to the civil rights movement and the anti-Vietnam war movement, and challenging to the faculty and their more traditional classmates.[113] They came to class and then left the building, since there was little room to socialize, study, or organize. The space that did exist did not invite one to stay. At some point during the sixties, with a combination of fondness and disgust, the students began to call the former "marvel of elegance" the "E Street Warehouse." Dean Paul Dean saw the future of the Law Center further east, near Union Station, and in 1971, Georgetown moved to McDonough Hall. Shortly thereafter, the Denson Building and all the annexes were demolished. Although Georgetown still owns the historic property at 5th and E Streets, an office building now occupies the site. Until recently, it was the home office of the Securities and Exchange Commission.

XVII

WINDOWS

OCTOBER 20, 2003

The glorious days of October have enabled us to recover some of the time lost to the rains of spring and summer. Roof membranes are being applied to both buildings and the mechanical penthouse on the roof of Hotung is nearly complete. The masonry work on the south side of Hotung is now complete, is progressing on the west side, and has just begun on the north side. On the east side, the masons have completed their work. The face brick is complemented by the architectural "eyebrow" over the second floor and the steel supports await the dramatic cornice that will overhang the roof. Face bricks have also reached the fourth floor on the west side of the Sport and Fitness Center, and we will soon begin to lay them on the south wall. To the north, the brick is climbing up the relief angles on the air shafts that will frame the glass curtain wall facing the green. We expect that all of the exterior work on both buildings will be completed in early January.

Work progresses on the interiors as well. CMU blocks now define the basketball court, the racquetball courts, and the locker rooms outside the pool. Scaffolding has been set, enabling workers to build the ceiling above the pool. Office walls up to the fifth floor in Hotung are defined by metal studs. Library shelf rails are in place. Door frames are appearing; elevator walls, rails, and machinery are being installed; and the pipes, ducts, and wires, soon to disappear from sight, continue to wrap the building. Perhaps the most visible signs of imminent exterior completion are the windows now being set in the Hotung Building. Office windows have been installed on the south and east sides. Soon the impressive multi-story windows and the dramatic arch windows will arrive.

Windows are seemingly everywhere in modern life. The double-hung sash and casement windows of our homes, the storefronts that liven our commercial corridors, and stunning and soaring design windows, such as those that billow out like blue-green sails from the new National Association of Realtors building on the New Jersey Avenue triangle add to our comfort, beckon us outward or inward, and play with our senses of sight and touch.

Arched window in the Wolff Library, Hotung Building
GEORGETOWN LAW CENTER ARCHIVE; SAM KITTNER, PHOTOGRAPHER

The modern world's love affair with windows and light is relatively new. The ancient world was at the mercy of weather, disease, stench, and war. Visible and invisible enemies hovered everywhere, taking lives, often without warning or explanation. Early men and women sought to seal themselves off from strangers and strange vapors rather than invite them in. The prophet Jeremiah, for example, warned that "death has come into our windows and entered our palaces."[114] Middle Eastern legend tells that Baal, the Canaanite god of fertility, objected to windows in his palace. After his arrogant designers ignored his warnings, Mot, the god of sterility, entered the palace "doing great harm."[115]

The history of windows is far more complex than our current familiarity and acceptance of them suggests. For this Construction Note, I relied heavily on the work of James Cross Giblin and his book called *Let There Be Light*.[116] The book was written for children, but provides wonderful descriptions and tales about windows in early civilizations. Twelve thousand years ago, windows were unknown. Nomads built their beehive-shaped huts from stones or slept in tepees and lean-tos made from branches and skins. Holes in their roofs allowed access and also dispersed smoke rising from a hearth. Windows served no purpose to the ancients. They let in weather and spirits, permitted enemy eyes to peer inside, and complicated the construction of dwellings that had to be erected, torn down, or abandoned quickly as the nomads moved from place to place.

Windows, though not as we know them, may have been developed by the Inuit people who lived in the far north of Canada. Living on the edge of glaciers, the Inuit would set translucent, freshwater ice blocks midway up the domes of their igloos. These "windows" let in light but still kept out the cold and roving prowlers of human, animal, or divine origin. The Inuit living away from the ice in branch homes often used translucent animal gut, bladders, or skins to the same effect.

As villages and small cities evolved in Mesopotamia around 6,000 B.C., permanent rectangular houses began to appear and windows became more important. Because cities permitted a collective defense against enemies, windows posed less danger that they did in nomadic times. Moreover, large numbers of people living in small and connected houses in warm climates required that more air flow into homes. Wall paintings from Egypt and reliefs from Assyria show openings in house walls covered with matting that could be rolled up or down as the weather required. In some places, thin slices of mica, selenite, or other varieties of gypsum provided a more permanent window barrier. Citizens of Crete in 2,000 B.C. had large windows and used transoms and mullions. Given the wealth of Crete, the windows were probably made from alabaster, but this, like so many other parts of Minoan culture, remains lost to modern research. While the people of Crete were looking out from their homes, the Greeks forswore windows to preserve their privacy. They built their homes as a series of single rooms with doors, but no windows, opening into great courtyards. Neither were windows placed in the outside walls of their homes. It is of no small cultural significance that the ancient Greek word the human eye meant the "window to the soul," connoting the privacy of thought and revealing, perhaps, another example of the relationship of architecture to many aspects of Greek life.

As they did with so many other architectural innovations, the Romans improved on the windows they found in other cultures. Glazed windows begin to appear in Imperial times. Fragments of greenish-blue glass set in bronze frames have been found in Pompeiian houses, and large clerestory windows, filled with shell, marble, mica, and perhaps glass, were used to retain heat in the Roman baths. The Romans also built greenhouses to raise crops in winter. Nonetheless, windows were not essential to most early Romans until they developed apartment buildings, some of which rose to six stories. In modest apartments, windows were usually covered by wood shutters, vellum, or oiled cloth. Better apartments featured mica or gypsum in the frames. By the second century A.D., glass was hardly a luxury. Bronze frames with nine-inch by twelve-inch panes of glass were in use throughout the Empire and glass-making became a major industry.

Windows appeared in the first century A.D. in China but the use of glass was late in developing. Instead, the Chinese made windows with wooden grills covered by silk paper. Later they made the paper for the windows from rags, tree bark, and plant stems. These windows reached Japan in the seventh century, where they developed into magnificent shoji screens, made with sliding wood panels and paper windows. These simple yet elegant screens still adorn homes in Japan today.

As the barbarians sacked the Roman Empire, they destroyed its glass windows and glass industry along with everything else. Europe returned to cloth, skin, and wooden window coverings. Castles and keeps rejected large windows and replaced them with slits in solid walls, large enough to permit arrows to fly but small enough to protect the archer. Nonetheless, windows did not completely disappear in medieval Europe. They continued to adorn both western and Byzantine churches. Hagia Sophia, built in Constantinople in 532 A.D., uses pierced marble frames with panes of glass.[117] Islamic builders in Egypt and Syria copied this technique but used cement instead of marble to gain greater technical freedom and hence, richness, in design.[118] They added small pieces of colored glass to produce brilliant light patterns. Because the climate was warm and dry in those regions, frames were also often left empty. The Islamic design patterns were subsequently copied in Europe in the twelfth and thirteenth century.[119] Using lead cames[120] and stained glass inserted into frames and mullions of stone instead of marble or cement, medieval builders and bishops ushered in an architectural explosion of Gothic cathedrals. Nobles, recognizing the richness of glass, slowly abandoned their fortified castles. Not until the 1500s, however, were England and France safe enough to turn the castles into chateaus and manor houses, built with proper windows for ventilation and light.[121] Large casement windows extending to the floor, commonly known as French doors, developed in the late Renaissance and became the standard window in Europe. Ancient fears had fallen away by then and the window became a permanent and welcome design element for the modern world.

The window designs in the Hotung International Building and the Sport and Fitness Center reflect this history, as well as the technological advances in theory and materials that have occurred since then. I will speak more about these technological advances in another Construction Note.

XVIII

THE EAST END

DECEMBER 8, 2003

As winter approaches, weather delays continue to menace our progress. Nonetheless, we hope to have the Hotung International Law Building sealed around the end of this year and the Sport and Fitness Center sealed shortly thereafter. The cornices now adorn all sides of the Hotung Building. Roof membranes cover both buildings and insulation is being installed for the roofs that cover the connecting halls between the Gewirz Residence Hall, the Sport and Fitness Center, and the Hotung International Building. Masonry has been completed on the Hotung Building and on all but the south wall of the Sport and Fitness Center. The majority of the windows have been installed in Hotung and they await application of the exterior mullion caps. Installation of the four-story glass curtain wall on the front of the Sport and Fitness Center will begin within the next few weeks.

When the exterior of a building is completed, progress becomes less obvious. We anxiously and impatiently wait to occupy the building, forgetting that there is still much to do inside. The interior block work for the Sport and Fitness Center is progressing and we can now see the outlines of the locker rooms and showers, the whirlpools and massage rooms, the racquetball courts, and the aerobic and spinning rooms. The ceiling lights are in place in the gym, awaiting the first tip-off or volley for serve. Wall, door, and soffit[122] framing continue, outlining the shapes of the various suites and offices in both buildings. Fire sprinkler main and branch lines run up to the third floor of both buildings. Conduit, cable, and wiring course through the walls, and compact shelving rails are set in the library floors. We can see where classes will occur — in the high-tech moot court, the seminar rooms, and the classrooms of Hotung. In the Sport and Fitness Center, the fireplace supports are hung, the fountain basins are poured, and the wine and coffee bar plumbing is set, awaiting quiet contemplation and social gatherings when classes are over. The coordination of all these systems defies a layman's understanding. Both the devil and the angel are in these details.

When the Law Center buildings and the National Association of Realtors building are completed, the neighborhood will bear no resemblance to the land

700 New Jersey Avenue, NW, site of the Williams Law Library
WILLIAM BARRETT, COURTESY KIPLINGER WASHINGTON COLLECTION

200-204 F Street, NW, site of the Georgetown Law Center's Tower Green
WILLIAM BARRETT, COURTESY KIPLINGER WASHINGTON COLLECTION

where Native Americans hunted and where streams and creeks swelled into swamps and marshes. All vestiges of post-Civil War life will also be gone. The history of this neighborhood, however, is rich, vibrant, and complex, reflecting the nineteenth and early twentieth century American experience. Before the Law Center moved to this neighborhood in 1971, European settlers, former slaves, and their descendants had lived here for almost two hundred years. When Washington City was carved out of Maryland in 1791, Benjamin Oden became the original proprietor of our land. During that time, it was called Bealls Levels. Later, it would be called the East End. Few people lived in the area during the first half of the nineteenth century. Early maps of our neighborhood show few buildings before 1850. Even when the Law School was founded in 1870, the land to the northeast of our present site remained rural and sparsely settled, due in part to the swamps surrounding the Tiber Creek.

Some of the earliest buildings in the neighborhood were started by George Washington in 1798, and completed shortly after he died. The houses, built at about North Capitol and Constitution Avenue, NE, remained standing until 1914.[123] The Baltimore and Ohio Railroad came to this area in 1835. The tracks ran though what is now Union Station and down Delaware Street before depositing travelers at New Jersey Avenue. In 1852, the B&O Railroad built a charming train station in the Italianate design at New Jersey Avenue between C and D Streets, NW, about where the Japanese-American memorial stands today. (See photo on page 66.) Abraham Lincoln, fearing a possible attack or kidnapping, arrived warily at this station to assume his Presidency in 1861. His funeral entourage departed from this same station in 1865, taking his body from a mourning Washington to his home in Illinois.

After a brief period of Northernization during the Civil War, Washington slowly returned to its Southern roots at the war's end. Attempts at integration, a main goal of the Reconstructionists, fell by the wayside after 1870.[124] De facto segregation in hotels, restaurants, hospitals, and theaters re-emerged. Southern congressmen fought for segregation in the public transit system. By 1906, Henry James would describe Washington as a place where "the North ceases to insist [and] the South may begin to presume."[125]

Class distinctions re-emerged as well, and were apparent in this neighborhood. Stephen Douglas built a house called Mount Julep (named for Douglas' partiality to whiskey), and two other homes in 1857 at 2nd and I Street, NW,[126] After the war, Generals Grant and Sherman joined Douglas as residents in what was then called Douglas Row. Sherman soon became a prominent resident of Washington and addressed a class of Georgetown Law students in 1873.[127] The wealthy continued to live even further west at Judiciary Square and Blagden Row, and in boarding houses and homes along C Street between 1st and 4th Streets, NW. Millard Fillmore, John Calhoun, Henry Clay, Francis Scott Key, John Fremont, and Thomas Hart Benton all resided in that neighborhood either before or after the war.

The Italianate B&O railway station, built in 1852 at New Jersey Avenue and C Street, NW
LIBRARY OF CONGRESS, PRINTS AND PHOTOGRAPHS DIVISION

To the northeast lived poor whites, recent immigrants, and African Americans who had moved north during and after the war. Land values to the north and east of our site were among the lowest in the city because of the swamps and marshes caused by the Tiber Creek. Until 1880, the only street paved in the northeast quadrant of D.C. was H Street, which linked Washington with the Bladensburg turnpike. The notorious Swampoodle neighborhood, a shantytown bounded by 1st Street, NW, and 2nd Street, NE, between G Street and K Street, NW, was home to poor, mostly Irish, immigrants. During the Civil War, soldiers were warned to stay out of the area because it was so dangerous. By 1880, it was well-known for crime, tuberculosis, typhoid, and malaria. Because of the rowdiness and mayhem of Swampoodle, the old No. 6 police station was located on New Jersey Avenue between D and E Streets, NW, just south of the existing fire station. The proximity of the police did not disturb one of the area's most successful crime organizations whose work was grisly but necessary for the advancement of medical science. At 419 New Jersey Avenue, where the Holiday Inn now stands, Maude Brown led a group of "resurrectionists," or body snatchers, who stole bodies from the city's burial grounds and then sold them to out-of-town medical schools.[128] Their exploits were uncovered and finally ended in 1894 when a barrel labeled "pork," but containing pickled human remains, was found in a warehouse at the B&O train station.[129]

The late nineteenth century was an era of tumult and growth in Washington, and this neighborhood experienced it all. Between 1870 and 1900, development brought many people and jobs to the neighborhood. Boss Shepherd brought corruption, or at least fiscal adventurism to Washington in the 1870s, but he also brought roads, streetlights, and sewers to the East End. Most of the Tiber Creek was enclosed in a sewer by 1877, although it was not completely tamed and consigned to the deep earth until 1907 when Union Station was built. Even professional baseball could be found in the area. From at least 1886 to 1892, the immortal Connie Mack played baseball for the Washington Nationals at Swampoodle Stadium.[130] Aficionados agree that home plate was at the corner of North Capitol Street and Massachusetts Avenue. Some people think that the third base line went up North Capitol Street and that centerfield was located where Union Station now stands. My own assessment of the existing photos of the park, (Not included in the book), showing Baltimore and Ohio Railroad trains and tracks in left field, favors instead a southern orientation, with the first base line going down North Capitol.[131] In either case, professional baseball would have returned nearly to its roots if Mayor Anthony Williams had succeeded in building a stadium for the new Washington Nationals at Florida Avenue and M Street, NE. As it is, Capitol Hill will have the team at Robert F. Kennedy (RFK) Stadium for a short while until a new stadium is built along the waterfront in southeast Washington.

Development did not bring prosperity to everyone. African Americans, who had enjoyed real freedom and opportunity during and just after the Civil War, found the grip of segregation tightening anew as the Southern culture of the city regained its pre-eminence. The concept of separate education for white and black children was affirmed by Congress in 1870.[132] Nativists and immigrants lived side by side but uneasily, always fearful of gang attacks. Nonetheless, jobs were available and communities began to develop. The M Street School, the first school for black students constructed with public funds, was built in the Romanesque style with colonial accents between 1890 and 1891 at M and 1st Street, NW.[133] It served as a high school until it was replaced by Dunbar, also in our neighborhood, in 1916. Between the two schools, they educated many of Washington's twentieth-century African-American intellectuals.[134] The M Street School became Perry Elementary School and educated students until the 1950s. It is now a community center at which Georgetown University undergraduate and law students volunteer. Many Irish and other Catholic children attended St. Aloysius Elementary School and Gonzaga High School. Gonzaga moved to North Capitol and I Streets, NE, in 1881 and remains a premier private school in the city. The Romanesque style Gales School, named after the eighth mayor of Washington, also opened in 1881 to serve white children in the neighborhood.[135] It continued to educate students until 1944. The Gales School building still stands across from the Law Center on the triangle north of Massachusetts Avenue at 1st Street, NW. It will soon be renovated and become a center for the care and assessment of abused and neglected children.

In 1856, the first Government Printing Office was opened at North Capitol and H Streets, NW. The current building was erected in 1903. Hotels such as the Commodore (now the Phoenix Park), the Dodge, the Continental, the Pennsylvania, the Capitol Park, the Bellevue (now the George), the Strathford (home to the Georgetown clinics in the 1980s, and next to the Capitol Plaza apartments which is the home to some law students today), and numerous boarding houses opened to serve the streams of people arriving at Union Station. New apartment houses, such as the Pierpont, the Navarre, and the Lundberg, were built where the highway now runs. Immigrants poured into the neighborhood after 1880, still the Irish but also the Italians who came to build the City Beautiful. Public buildings, such as the Library of Congress Jefferson Building (built in 1897) and Union Station (built in 1907), and Washington's beautiful cathedrals all felt the touch of the Italian masons' skilled hands. New parishes and congregations were formed. St. Aloysius Church was completed in 1859 at North Capitol and I Streets, NW. A German parish, St. Mary Mother of God, opened at 7th and G Streets, NW, in the early 1900s.[136] Holy Rosary was formed in 1913 in a house at 83 H Street, NW, to serve the Italian immigrants.[137] The pastor, Reverend Nicholas De Carlo, was instructed to minister only to Italians and to forbid English-speaking people from attending Mass.[138] Holy Rosary's new church, still standing across the highway from the Law Center, was built between 1919 and 1923 with a rectory behind it. Holy Rosary's rectory, now moved to the south side of the church, figured prominently in our ability to close F Street in 2003 for the Campus Completion Project. The church bell tower, the mosaics, and the interior decorations were all added in the late 1920s. This parish quickly became the center of East End social life and continues to be a thriving parish today. Second Baptist built its church at 3rd and H Streets, NW, in 1898. Washington's oldest synagogue, Adas Israel, was built between 1873 and 1876 at 600 5th Street, NW. That building was moved to 3rd and G Streets, NW, in 1969. It is now a museum of Jewish heritage. In the early 1900s, three synagogues operated between 5th and 8th Streets on I Street, NW. Jewish merchants from the East End, including my wife's ancestors, joined the merchants from 7th Street as they walked to Shabbat services, literally closing I Street on Friday nights.[139]

By 1923, the area was completely developed. Small factories, hotels, apartment buildings, and flat-front houses stood side by side in this multicultural working-class neighborhood. Looking at the neighborhood now, one can hardly believe that this was a thriving residential area, teeming with small businesses. Vaccaro's Italian Delicatessen and Bakery survived at 3rd Street and Massachusetts Avenue, NW, until the 1970s. Each morning, trucks laden with bread left the Holmes Bakery with their morning deliveries. The Holmes Bakery was owned by relatives of the wife of the Law Center's Professor Jack Murphy. Holmes stood about where the new Sport and Fitness Center stands. During the excavation of the site, we found remnants of the old Madison Alley that connected 1st and 2nd Streets, NW, and provided the exit route for the Holmes drivers. Viareggio's

Grocery Store stood at 3rd and I Streets, NW. My in-laws' relatives ran a grocery store on 1st and E Streets, NW, just south of the Law Center campus. One of the few remaining examples of the area's residential architecture stands on E Street between 1st and 2nd Streets, NW, vacant and a silent reminder of the laughing children and struggling families who lived here in another time. There is no doubt that this deteriorating building will be torn down in the near future. A few other such houses still stand north of Massachusetts Avenue on 3rd Street, NW. These solid middle-class houses often occupied the same blocks as notoriously squalid and overcrowded alley houses. Although construction of alley housing was prohibited after 1892, the very poor occupied them here and throughout the city until the Franklin Roosevelt administration.[140]

The people of this neighborhood were a melange of nationalities, with the Irish, English, German, Swedes, Italians, and Eastern European Jews mixing relatively peacefully with African Americans until the 1950s. Between 1950 and 1970, these communities were all swept away. Because of ill-managed urban renewal and a planned inner-city highway system that nearly destroyed L'Enfant's dreams, the neighborhood became a wasteland. In 1971, Georgetown Law Center became the pioneer that brought life back to the area. By 2004, stories will again resonate from this thriving urban neighborhood. But the history of our site is not yet complete. The stories of the demise and subsequent rise of this area will appear in future Construction Notes.

XIX

WINDOWS REDUX

JANUARY 30, 2004

Every construction project has milestones that measure its progress. Topping off, completing the masonry, sealing the building, finishing the duct work, and other such events are noted and celebrated, giving us a chance to pause and ponder at the combination of mind and might, math and mud, that ultimately results in a functional work of art which may stand for centuries. Although the vagaries of the weather have left us slightly behind schedule, we recently celebrated one of those milestones in the Campus Completion Project, and will soon celebrate another. The Bennu scaffolding has been removed from the south side of the Sport and Fitness Center, signaling the completion of the masons' work. One hundred and forty thousand bricks were laid in Hotung and another 150,000 were set in Sport and Fitness. If piled one on top of the other, they would reach over 54,000 feet into the air, slightly lower than the altitude of the Concorde in flight. If laid out one next to the other, they would set a path to the door of Camden Yards in Baltimore.[141]

Once our bricks were laid and the walls washed down, the scaffolding was dismantled, bringing us one step closer to a completed building. Scaffolds have been used to build walls for centuries. Artwork from a thousand years ago shows wood or bamboo scaffolding scaling up the sides of buildings, battlements, and statues. Today, thousands of feet of pipe scaffolding are sold or leased every day in all parts of the developed world for the same purposes. On our project, we have used this traditional pipe scaffolding called "scaffolding in place" to build the west wall of Hotung and the east and west walls of Sport and Fitness and to install their windows. For the remaining walls, we have used the more modern "mast climbing work platforms" manufactured by the Bennu Company of Canada. These yellow towers, connected by steel beam platforms, lift workers and materials up the sides of buildings, permitting both to reach their place of work quickly and safely.

According to *Masonry Magazine*, mast climbers were developed in Europe in the 1970s and first appeared in the U.S. in 1982 in St. Paul, Minnesota.[142] Originally powered by electricity, the mast climbers are now powered by gasoline

Benno Scaffolding climbing up the east side of the Hotung Building
WHITING TURNER CONSTRUCTION PHOTO; BOB CREAMER, PHOTOGRAPHER

engines. These mast climbers have heavier load capacities and faster installation times than traditional "scaffolding in place." The fast elevator speeds generate high efficiency, safety, and productivity in the masonry trades. They also fascinate construction site onlookers as the platforms literally climb up the sides of a building. Mast climbers usually rise up to thirty-five feet in the air without being tied to a building and up to 800 feet when anchored to a wall.[143] On our buildings, they have reached a height of seventy-four feet. A mast climbing platform can extend up to sixty feet between its support columns, as those on our project did. Climbing platforms can also be bridged together, permitting workers to move easily along an entire span of a building. Mast climbers have revolutionized the masonry industry and were essential to maintaining our construction schedule. Had we used only "scaffolding in place," the unfavorable weather would have placed us far behind schedule. Although the absence of the mast climbers on our site signifies progress, I note their departure with just a tinge of regret.

A second milestone will be the sealing of the buildings. Only a few of Hotung's taller window openings remain empty. They will be soon filled with soaring three-story windows that will complete the building's dramatic exterior design. Within a few weeks, the stunning glass curtain wall of the Sport and Fitness Center will be completed as well. In both cases, the power and clarity of the buildings' designs become apparent as the windows fill the openings in the facades. Once the buildings are sealed, they can be heated and work can begin on the interior finishes.

Early in the design process, the Committee and the Shepley Bulfinch architects decided to make the Hotung Building and the Sport and Fitness Center appear very different from one another. We did so to reflect their different uses and to create a strong sense of identity for the donors. The sizes of the windows signal the kinds of activity occurring within a particular area of the building. Large-size windows signify areas that are open and occupied by many people, such as classrooms, lobbies, exercise rooms, and reading rooms. Narrower windows denote individual offices or places of individual study. The arched windows in Hotung, a building with a traditional academic purpose, recall the vestigial arch from the Law Center's home from 1890 to 1971, now destroyed, at 5th and E Streets, NW. As mentioned earlier, that entry arch now sits in the Library Quad, a visual connection between our past and our present.

Hotung's articulated panes of glass (some panes are forward of others) offer a rhythm and vitality to the facade by creating shadows in an otherwise very large surface. The floor-to-ceiling glass curtain wall in the Sport and Fitness Center conveys a more contemporary and playful tone, suggesting its more relaxed purpose. It provides a welcoming invitation to those outside and brings natural light to the inside. This glass wall was designed to take advantage of the new Tower Green that will separate McDonough Hall from the new buildings. The ground level interior of Sport and Fitness is designed to complement the stone patio that sits between the curtain wall and the Green. A fourth-floor terrace, adjacent to the basketball court, provides a place to cool down after a game. The inside/outside effect created by the glass curtain wall serves to unify the relaxed atmosphere of the interior and exterior spaces and visually connects all of the buildings surrounding the Tower Green.

Windows have had a great influence on American architecture. Indeed, late Tudor commercial policies concerning glass affected the exploration and settlement of the New World. Elizabeth I held the monopoly on glass production in England.[144] Her most loyal supporters installed large windows in their palaces to show support (both political and financial) for the monarch. Tourists visiting stately English homes today will notice that palaces from the Elizabethan era have larger and more expansive windows than buildings from any other period of English history except the modern. The demand for glass, however, surpassed Elizabeth's ability to produce it as the timber used to fire her furnaces ran out. Much of the seventeenth-century English woodland had been cut down for energy, and coal was only then emerging as a source to power the furnaces. Moreover, few Englishmen were skilled in glassmaking. Thus, much of England's glass had to be imported from other regions of Europe.[145]

Elizabeth saw the New World as an energy resource for her furnaces. To that end, she sent Polish and German glassmakers to the Jamestown colony in 1608 to produce glass.[146] These artisans produced the first factory-made products on the North America continent. For reasons that remain obscure, this first attempt to create a glass-making industry failed. Another was organized in 1622, but the imported Italian glassmakers "fell extremely sick" and the venture ceased by 1624.[147] Nonetheless, the introduction of coal to fire the English furnaces reinvigorated the glass industry. The first successful colonial glass-making industry was developed in New Jersey in 1739.[148] Glass windows became common during the eighteenth and nineteenth centuries, and the English vertical-sliding sash window and the double-hung window became the standard in the United States.

The "industrial glass" entry of the *Encyclopedia Britannica* has comprehensive information on the history and development of glass and provided much of the detail for this section.[149] The glass for windows is made from silica, such as sand, mixed with soda ash and lime. The mixture liquefies when heated to 1,500 degrees centigrade and then solidifies as glass when cooled. No one knows who invented glass, but some disputed legends attribute its discovery to Phoenician sailors.[150] Early European glass did not resemble the glass we use today. Most early window glass was produced by the "crown process," developed by the Normans in the Middle Ages. Crown glass is produced by blowing a mass of glass into a globe at the end of the blowing iron that is then marvered to a conical shape. "A pontil rod [is] then attached to the other end and the blowing iron [is] cracked off, leaving a jagged opening." The glassmaker then places the globe into the "glory hole" (the mouth) of the furnace and reheats it, all the while spinning the soft glass to keep it from sagging. "At some point, centrifugal force [from the spinning motion] causes the globe to flash into a flat disk, which grows larger as the spinning continues. Upon cooling, the disk [is] cracked off the pontil rod." The glass produced by the "crown method" is not truly flat. Concentric circular waves emanate from a thick center. In the middle of the disk is the crown, the point where the pontil formerly was attached. The crown method could not produce large sheets of glass but it did create panes large enough for early windows. Many buildings remaining from the colonial era still have windows made from the crown method. Such glass is prized today, especially if it is original. Today, however, it is used as a decorative element rather than a functional one.

Broad glass was developed in medieval times using a process that continued to be used with variations into the twentieth century. Broad glass is created by repeatedly gathering, blowing, and swinging molten glass until it forms a large cylinder. These cylinders would often be as much as fifty centimeters in diameter and 175 centimeters long. "The cylinder [is] slit when cold and then gradually opened with moderate reheating to become flat. Glass made from this process was flatter than crown glass and did not have the telltale crown in the middle; moreover, it could be made in much larger pieces. The use of compressed air in the early 1900s allowed the cylinders to be blown as large as seventy five centimeters in diameter and up to nine meters in length. Despite its advantages over crown glass, broad glass had surface waviness and variations in thickness." A higher degree of flatness could be obtained if the glass was cast on a steel table and rolled. These glass plates were then ground and polished. Using the Bicheroux process, "introduced in Germany in the 1920s, about a ton of glass was melted in a pot and carried to the table, where it was poured through a pair of rollers. Rolling the sheet reduced the amount of grinding needed for flatness."

At the dawn of the twentieth century, Emile Fourcault of Belgium and Irving Colburn of the Libbey-Owens Glass Company in Charleston, West Virginia, each invented a process that greatly improved the glass rolling process. Nonetheless, like glass from earlier processes, theirs had to be ground and polished for optical clarity. Finally in 1959, Alastair Pilkington introduced a float glass process in England that eliminated the need for grinding and polishing.

The windows Shepley Bulfinch chose for our buildings are made from two-pane, four-surface, insulated glass. The panes are clear although they have the slightly greenish cast that is typical in glass. Our glass has a "Low E" coating that reduces heat loss and heat gain through the window. The coating is transparent and is placed on the inside face of the outside glass. "Low E" rated glass reduces energy consumption and costs by reducing the loads on the heating and air conditioning systems. A vacuum is created between the two panes to prevent fogging and the accumulation of condensation on the interior surfaces between the two panes of the glass.

The window frames and the window mullions are also insulated. Mullions are the vertical and horizontal dividers in windows. The frames and the mullions are assembled from about half a dozen pieces of extruded aluminum. These hold the glass in place and provide a framework to attach the windows to the wall. Because they are made from metal, the frames expand and contract depending on weather conditions. This expansion and contraction could permit water to seep into the frame and to hold condensation that might infiltrate the window system. To allow moisture to drain from the frame, weep holes are placed on the underside of the mullions and in the windowsill. To minimize condensation further, the cavities on the inside of the frames and the mullions are filled with insulation. The insulation prevents the accumulation of condensation on the inside faces of the frames and mullions that results when the temperature on the outside of the window is at a different level from the temperature on the inside of the window. Such condensation can lead to the formation of mold and an unhealthy interior environment. A simple and common example of heat transference and its subsequent condensation occurs when beads of water form on the outside of a glass of iced tea on a hot day.

Attaching the windows to the wall is also critical to reducing heat transfer. The walls of our buildings are masonry, while the window frames are metal. The two materials expand and contract at different rates, creating a vulnerable zone where the two meet. Consequently, the joint between the masonry and the metal must be flexible enough to allow movement but strong enough to prevent the windows from being knocked or blown out. A structural engineer designs the connection to allow this seeming contradiction of stability and flexibility. Since the wall assembly and the window assembly are both insulated, the joint between the two must also be insulated, otherwise air or moisture will penetrate the building. The infiltrating air would cause drafts and render the HVAC systems ineffective. The moisture could also cause mold.

The windows are also engineered to withstand pressure changes. Evolving weather systems and wind movement around a building cause the air pressure inside and outside of a building to be different. In addition, the air pressure near the corners of a building is often different from the air pressure at its center. To endure the pressure differential, the windows and frames must be sturdy, yet flexible.

Once the windows are fabricated and brought to the site, they are bolted into place. The joint between the window and the wall is covered with the blue sheet rubberized air barrier that I described in an earlier note. The barrier overlaps the sprayed-on air barrier between the face brick and the concrete block backup. The barrier then folds into a special compartment of the window frame creating a seal. The joint is stuffed with insulation and caulked on both the inside and the outside of the joint.

The amount of physical labor and mental ingenuity that goes into designing and installing a modern window system is astounding. Windows must please the eye, but they also affect the senses of touch, smell, and sound. To most people, windows seem like simple devices that let air and light in but keep intruders out. As in times past, those intruders are both visible and invisible. Now, however, we understand them with a much greater level of sophistication. Centuries of thought and labor have taken these simple objectives of light and protection to levels of intense design, planning, and implementation. These engineering advances have combined with our designer's art to create two of only a handful of buildings that will be certified by the Air Barrier Association of America as true air barrier buildings. The windows are a critical element in the air barrier assembly. The air barrier design will make the our buildings more comfortable, lead to a substantial reduction in energy use, and result in buildings that are hostile to pathogens and intruders.

With the sealing of the buildings, the exteriors will be completed. Our activity will turn to the interiors and the Tower Green. We are issuing contracts for security systems and telecommunication systems. We are picking colors for the walls and carpets, locks for the doors, and fabrics for the furniture. We are making final design changes to the dining area and the retail space. Our landscape plan, anchored by a clock tower that identifies our campus as an academic center within a vibrant urban neighborhood, is almost complete. The dreams of former Dean Paul Dean and his successors are approaching a reality.

XX

THE URBAN GHOST TOWN

MARCH 12, 2004

Although we had hoped to have both new buildings sealed by now, their major entrances still await doors and windows. Installation of the arched curtain wall of the west entrance to Hotung is under way, however, and work will begin shortly on the east entrance. The glass curtain wall of the Sport and Fitness Center is also nearly complete, although its complicated entrance required some structural redesign. We have also taken the first steps in designing the Tower Green. A fifty-five-foot clock tower will anchor the landscape design. Excavation for the tower is complete and the concrete footings and the foundation walls have been poured. Other significant tasks are under way, although many take place outside the view of the casual observer. Gas lines are now connected, allowing temporary heating units to operate inside the building. As a result, the installation of interior walls and finishes has begun in earnest. The building waterlines have been tied into the twelve-inch water main so that plumbing systems can be tested. Sewer line tie-ins will occur shortly. Contracts for exercise equipment, furniture, security, and technology are being issued. Architects have been retained to redesign the first floor of the Williams Library when the international law collection moves to the Hotung Building in the summer.

The interior block walls in the Sport and Fitness Center are almost complete. The aerobic and spinning rooms are clearly identifiable. Walls now separate the two racquetball courts from the basketball court. Frames to support the lockers are being installed and the whirlpools are poured and plumbed. Shower basins are in place and ceramic tile is being installed throughout the entire locker room complex.

The seating tiers have been framed in the mid-sized classrooms in the Hotung International Building, and the seminar rooms on the fifth and sixth floors are clearly identifiable. Most of the faculty, library, and program offices are framed and drywalled, so the alumni visitor center, the International Programs Office, and the Continuing Legal Education offices are defined. The glass and stainless steel railings on the monumental stairway leading to the new International Law

Library are in place. The two main elevators are operational and their stainless steel doors await our first visitors. Four other elevators will come on line soon.

Georgetown's campus will soon be the jewel of our East End neighborhood. As you may have read in last Sunday's *Washington Post*, "the once-desolate East End is bustling with new life."[151] Condos and apartments bring new residents while shops, restaurants, and theaters re-establish the area as a commercial engine of the city. The map of the East End that appeared in the *Post* showed the eastern boundary of the neighborhood at the Interstate 395 ditch; but citizens with longer memories know that the original East End boundary was North Capitol Street, thus encompassing our property as well.

The desolation from which we are recovering can be traced back to the 1950s. Its roots, however, go deeper into history. The East End and the former neighborhood just to the north, sometimes called Northwest 1, were populated mostly by working-class African Americans and European immigrants. Although wealthy and prominent people like Stephen Douglas, Ulysses Grant, and William Tecumseh Sherman once lived near 2nd and I Streets, NW, the area never became fashionable. As the grip of segregation tightened in Washington after 1870, the few wealthy citizens in our neighborhood moved to the northwest sections of the city. Those who remained often struggled economically and socially, with help coming primarily from the area churches.

422 2nd Street, N.W. and the surrounding area, circa late 1950s
WILLIAM BARRETT, COURTESY KIPLINGER WASHINGTON COLLECTION

Residential neighborhoods north of Massachusetts Avenue deteriorated in the era between 1890 and 1950. Referring to that era and that neighborhood, local newspapers described a "half-century of decay and neglect"[152] producing "slums, crime, and degradation." They called the neighborhood a "menace — the veritable sink of iniquity." The area around Holy Rosary parish avoided much of this desolation until after World War II, but the Northwest 1 neighborhood across Massachusetts Avenue suffered greatly throughout the era. Racism and the depressions of the late 1870s, the early 1890s, and the 1930s exacerbated the misery of the people living there. Moreover, restrictive real estate provisions forced the increasing number of African Americans moving to the area from the South into already overcrowded and substandard housing. Although new employment opportunities were created during World Wars I and II, African Americans usually had access only to the lower-paying positions. As those jobs were filled, the new residents streaming in from the South had few options.

The infamous 2nd police district, stretching from Massachusetts Avenue to Florida Avenue and from Union Station to 14th Street, NW, was a neighborhood of "rotting hovels, rusted tin fences, and littered yards." Called the "Sinful Second" or the "Wickedest Precinct," it housed the worst slums in Washington, D.C. Flats and tenements were built "side by side and back to back."[153] It was an area where "sunlight was a stranger." By 1950, one-half of the houses were dilapidated, without plumbing, and without adequate heat or light.[154] People in the area often lived six to a room. Housing codes were seldom enforced, either out of pity for the residents who had nowhere else to go or because of graft. Social services, then as now, were under-funded and poorly staffed. Every other child in the area was illegitimate under the laws of that day, and the tuberculosis and alcoholism rates were the highest in the city.[155]

Thirty courts or alleys, with names like Logan, Marion or Clothesline, infamous for one vice or another, laced the neighborhood. Crime was rampant. One could buy "with ease a shot of dope, a numbers play, a woman, a jug of Sneaky Pete on ice and all the stolen merchandise you want. Make a wrong remark and you [could] get your throat cut for free."[156] Although the precinct's 1953 crime rate of nineteen murders, 269 robberies and 714 house breakings seems low today,[157] it was a scandal for that era. The police call box at 6th and N Streets, NW, was the busiest box in the city.[158]

The reasons for this slide within this otherwise thriving international city were as common then as they are today. Budget strangulation by a Congress unwilling to appropriate an adequate federal payment, the lack of meaningful home rule, and the pervasiveness of racism in an essentially Southern city virtually guaranteed the result. Moreover, the post-World War II boom spurred on by the GI Bill and housing policies that benefited whites more than blacks resulted in a flight of the middle class from the city to the suburbs. Even after attorney Ralph Urciolo, a Holy Rosary parishioner, teamed with legendary African-American lawyer Charles Houston to attack restrictive housing covenants in the D.C. courts, city planners were still looking for ways to keep neighborhoods segregated.[159] Urciolo and Houston eventually prevailed when the Supreme Court declared restrictive covenants unconstitutional in *Shelley v. Kraemer*,[160] a case with which theirs was joined for Court consideration. Nonetheless, their victory had little immediate effect on segregation in the city. The federal committees that ruled Washington, D.C., were often led by Congressmen from Southern states who found little political advantage in ameliorating the causes of poverty, especially since the urban poverty in Washington affected citizens who did not look like the voters in the Congressmen's hometowns.[161] By the mid-1950s, the combination of these policies and practices had devastated Northwest 1 and spilled over into the East End.

Calls for urban renewal to relieve the plight of those living in poverty began in the late 1940s and came to fruition in the late 1950s and early 1960s. Plans were made to build new parks, improve commercial areas, and close the dangerous streets and alleys. North Capitol Street was to become a "dignified and beautiful" approach to the Capitol. But the early plans, issued by Ulysses S. Grant III, grandson of the hero of the Civil War, also reinforced the practice of segregated housing. The first urban renewal site was the old Southwest neighborhood, a small enclave of mostly black and some poor white residents living between the Potomac and Anacostia Rivers and Independence Avenue.[162] The plan called for the complete destruction of the neighborhood and the permanent relocation of its residents to the other side of the Anacostia River. By the time the bulldozers were through, there was nothing left of the old neighborhood. The total devastation of Southwest produced calls for something different in the Northwest Urban Renewal District. The original plan for the 2nd precinct called for razing all 16,000 houses and relocating the 60,000 people who lived there. Neighborhood outcries produced new plans, intense debates, and more new plans and challenges. The City issued "raze or repair"[163] orders against many dwellings hoping to force some resolution of the issue. Ultimately most of the early urban renewal plans were abandoned. During the past thirty years, housing policies changed and new residents moved into the area. Today, homes in the 2nd precinct's Shaw and Logan Circle neighborhoods, once called "rotting hovels," now sell for hundreds of thousands of dollars.

The final plan for Northwest 1, an area within the larger Northwest Urban Renewal tract bounded by Union Station to the east and I-395 to the west, and Massachusetts Avenue to the south and M Street to the north, called for the demolition of 1,011 homes and the displacement of over 7,000 people. Although some houses were rehabilitated, most were torn down. The few residents who remained could walk out their front door to a view of the Capitol that was unimpeded by other buildings.

Many buildings on the land we currently own were also torn down. At one time the City planned to build a thirty-one-unit mobile home park on our McDonough Hall site, but I can find no evidence that the plan was carried out. Some time later, a similar park for 225 units was planned along New Jersey Avenue between Prince and L Streets.

Some hope actually emerged out of all this human and architectural desolation. Officials from Mt. Airy Baptist Church, Bible Way Church, and the Prince Hall Masons formed nonprofit organizations that built Sibley Plaza and Tyler House, two mid-rise apartment buildings on North Capitol Street for low- and moderate-income families. The Golden Rule Apartments soon followed. A group of Catholics from Gonzaga High School and St. Aloysius Church formed a nonprofit group to build a low- and moderate-income housing community called Sursum Corda, Latin for "lift up your hearts." Built between 1967 and 1969, the townhouses and apartments featured air conditioning, garbage disposals, and washers and dryers. The concept for these houses and apartments grew out of socially progressive ideas of the 1960s and 1970s to provide affordable, quality housing to poor residents who had been displaced by urban renewal. A group of nuns moved into the neighborhood to provide spiritual and temporal assistance to the residents, some of whom lived in the neighborhood before the demolition began. At the time, an editorial in the *Washington Post* lauded the architects for building "a compact little village."[164]

But the hope generated by these projects soon turned to bitterness. Urban renewal stalled, and white flight produced an even more segregated city. Instead of model communities, urban renewal had produced total devastation in the Southwest Urban Renewal area and "a low-income segregated ghetto without adequate schools, shopping or community facilities" in Northwest 1. Recent stories in the *Washington Post* tell that the residents of Sursum Corda continue to suffer from the debilitating effects of the well-intentioned but misguided and poorly planned efforts of the 1950s and 1960s.[165] The last of the many nuns who once lived at Sursum Corda moved out when their home became a target for crime.[166] Today, however, developers are competing to buy the land, offering large sums of money, to the current owners. In November, 2005, the 167 remaining families agreed to a deal that would give each $80,000, half the profits on the sale of 500 condominiums, and the promise of a new home.[167]

Many of the homes south of Massachusetts Avenue were torn down because of urban renewal, but no new housing was built here. When the Law Center began purchasing land in 1965, few vestiges of this once-thriving neighborhood remained. No buildings stood on the McDonough Hall site. The Salvation Army and a few other small commercial buildings stood south of F Street where the Gewirz Residence Hall now stands, and a few townhouses remained on the Williams Library site. To the west, land was being cleared for the Center Leg Freeway. The Italians of Holy Rosary had moved to the suburbs, although they remained active in their church. The hotels near Union Station had long lost their glory, as airplanes replaced trains as the major form of transportation. By 1965, the hotels had deteriorated into dingy waystations. Urban renewal, once thought of as a cure for the city's poverty, had instead created an urban ghost town in the East End. It would take the foresight of Dean Paul Dean and his colleagues at Georgetown to begin the long, but now successful, rejuvenation of our neighborhood.

McDonough Hall, designed by Edward Durell Stone
GEORGETOWN LAW CENTER ARCHIVE; HOLLY EATON, PHOTOGRAPHER

XXI

MCDONOUGH HALL

APRIL 23, 2004

The last of the exterior elements of the Hotung International Law Building and Georgetown Sport and Fitness Center are being set into place. The east entrance of Hotung and the north entrance of Sport and Fitness are nearly complete. The last of the windows have been installed on the south walls, and spandrel glass covers most of the otherwise visible beams. Mullion covers are being installed on both buildings and louvers hide the air shafts and mechanical rooms.

The interiors change daily. Most of the door frames are set in their drywall partitions. Blocking and plywood are being installed in the servery of the cyber cafe, and vanity tops and millwork are starting to appear throughout the buildings. Interior architectural motifs are emerging. The first section of the terrazzo floor, angled towards the curve of the facade and the main entrance, has been poured on the second floor of Sport and Fitness. Design walls have also been erected, similarly oriented towards the door. The decorative mill-worked walls of Hotung's moot court offer glimpses of our intention to mimic the interior of the Supreme Court. Gleaming stainless steel elevator doors peek through their protective coverings, and the cherry-finished library circulation desk gives hints of the rich textures of Hotung's interior palette. Ceiling grids and light fixtures are being mounted and are visible from the outside. Walls on several floors of the Sport and Fitness Center are already painted, and tile floors are being grouted in the bathrooms. Air handling units, gas lines, and plumbing fixtures are being tested throughout both buildings, all working as intended.

On the Tower Green along the old F Street right-of-way, concrete support walls have been poured for the clock tower, showing the cutout for the four-sided clock. The tower's precast concrete base has been attached, and the first course of bricks has been laid. This steady but accelerating pace of work reminds us that the campus completion is nearly at hand.

It has taken almost forty years to build this campus and to fulfill the dreams of former Dean Paul R. Dean and his colleagues. In 1962, Dean described the old "E Street Warehouse," the Law Center's complex of buildings at 5th and E Streets, NW, as "unquestioningly...the least adequate of any of the major law schools in the country."[168] The library was housed on thirteen floors of three separate buildings; the dormitories no longer met minimum standards for safety, and the expansion of the evening and graduate curricula was hampered by a lack of space. Dean realized that the Law Center's future could not be assured without a new facility. In 1965, he announced that he had purchased, for $2.3 million, 82,000 square feet of land six blocks from the United States Capitol and four blocks from the judicial center of Washington.[169] Although the old arguments about moving to the Georgetown main campus arose anew, the Law Center's historic commitment to the center city remained intact. Dean retained a world-class architect, Edward Durell Stone, to design a building that would accommodate 1,675 students, seventy-five faculty, 21,000 square feet of classroom space, a moot court, and 50,000 square feet of library space. Dean reported that "the new building [would] liberate the Law Center from the physical and academic inefficiencies [of the] present maze of buildings which grew in a casual unintegrated manner, and which have constituted in the past obstacles of crippling proportions to student and faculty research."[170]

Paying for the building was not a simple matter. The budget for the building was projected to be $11,000,000. Alumni donors and federal grants and loans were needed to finance the building. At that time, fundraising for the Law Center was not a major university priority and the Law Center itself had no separate development staff. Indeed, before 1965, no one had ever made a one-million-dollar gift to the university, let alone to the Law Center. But dreams are often fulfilled in surprising ways. Help came from two remarkable men who had experienced Georgetown in very different ways. Despite these differences, they shared a belief in the Law Center's educational mission that was pivotal to the emerging campus we see today.

In 1934, Lyndon Baines Johnson, then working for a congressman on Capitol Hill, entered Georgetown Law School as an evening student.[171] He wanted to study law "to better [his] mental processes, to prepare [him] to earn an honest and respectable living, and possibly qualify [him] to make some contribution to society."[172] Although the pace of his work on the Hill and his recent marriage to Lady Bird forced him to withdraw before he even sat for his first examinations, he retained ties to his "almost alma mater." That was fortunate. When a funding freeze threatened a loss of federal funds for Georgetown's new building project, then President Lyndon Johnson told an aide to "call them up down there and tell them to take the damn freeze off the grant to my alma mater."[173]

The other man, like Johnson, sparked both admiration and controversy during his career. Bernard P. McDonough never boasted about his academic work at Georgetown Law Center. He entered in 1925 and often said he "finished last in his class."[174] His biographer, Eugene Murdock, wrote that McDonough was a practical man who "never sat for the bar exam and actually developed an antipathy toward lawyers."[175] Nonetheless, he valued the logic that the study of law provided. McDonough was a late bloomer whose business success was slow but steady. He built his fortune on "shoes and cement, shovels and concrete, hotels

ion will reveal that the bricks of McDonough, Gewirz, Hotung, and Sport
ness are all similar yet slightly different from one another, providing an
ed palette without being redundant.

fusion of purpose and material, dreams and style, remains a powerful
n American education and architecture. Georgetown's campus began with
and a clearly defined purpose. It has been enhanced through architectur-
and material. The architecture of each of the Law Center buildings speaks
chool's dreams and purpose. McDonough Hall brought a permanence of
r academic excellence in this neighborhood. It did so with a modernist
ural statement of power and forthrightness that embodied Paul Dean's
f a modern Law Center, built on a bedrock of excellence and justice. Our
ldings continue that dream, in architectural styles that harken back to
pose, but open us to an urban vibrancy that is returning to our neigh-
and to a community of nations of which we are an indivisible part.

and barges."[176] He was fifty-two when he first considered himself wealthy and
was sixty-six when his financial empire, the Marmac corporation of Parkersburg,
West Virginia, was completed. He had boundless energy and a passion for work.
"Business was both his work and his play."[177] "His mind was like a dynamo, powering a network of activities in dozens of places."[178] "He was tough, demanding,
driving, intense, and impatient with inefficiency and insubordination;"[179] but he
was loyal to people and to places that helped him along the way. McDonough
had always been a contributor to Georgetown's alumni fund and had been a
member of the Board of Regents. He was interested in the new building and told
Dean that he wanted to do "something big." At a lunch at the Mayflower Hotel,
McDonough offered Dean one million dollars for the Law Center's new building. At the time, it was the largest gift ever given to Georgetown. In return, the
Board of Directors named the new building the Bernard P. McDonough Hall.

The architect Dean chose to design the building, Edward Durell Stone, was
once described by *Time* magazine as "a pioneer modernist" and "one of the profession's freest spirits and by general consensus the most versatile designer and
draftsman of his generation."[180] The passing of time has not been as generous to
Stone's legacy as *Time* magazine was. Stone began his career as an apprentice for
Coolidge, Shepley, Bulfinch, and Abbott, the firm started by H. H. Richardson
and a forerunner of our current design firm. In the early 1930s, he started his
own practice, designing residential buildings in the International Style,[181] an austere "modern" style of architecture featuring reinforced concrete, steel, glass
block, and strip windows. This sleek, spare style abandoned ornamentation and
lavish materials. By the 1950s, Stone had totally repudiated this modernist style,
comparing it to "the latest model automobile, doomed to early obsolescence."[182]
Following the lead of Frank Lloyd Wright, Stone began to see the importance of
a building's site to the style of his architecture. His approach, still "modernist"
but with more decorative elements, first appeared in hotel and academic architecture in the 1940s. It was decisively displayed in his stunning design of the U.S.
Embassy in New Delhi. Its rectangular shape and temple-like form anticipated
both the Kennedy Center and Georgetown's McDonough Hall.

Stone's work featured pierced screen walls, non-load bearing partitions
behind structural members, overhanging canopies to provide shade and breezeways, and platforms that hid automobiles, created garden areas, and provided
monumental settings. These stylistic elements appear in Stone buildings at
Harvey Mudd College, the University of Chicago, the U.S. Naval Academy, and
many other universities. Stone also employed these elements in many public
buildings in cities around the country. In Washington, three Stone buildings bear
these features: the National Geographic Society Building, the John F. Kennedy
Center for the Performing Arts, and Georgetown's McDonough Hall.

Stone worked for more than eight years on the Kennedy Center, providing
two concepts for the building. Unfortunately, the first and better design proved
too costly.[183] The Kennedy Center we visit today is his second attempt to integrate the banks of the Potomac into the building's design. He emphasized the

view of the Potomac, creating a grand foyer that simultaneously provides access to the three auditoria and to an equally grand terrace overlooking the river. Tall columns separated from the frame of the huge, rectangular, white marble building, support Stone's typical overhanging flat roof. These columns do not harken to the neoclassical columns of triumphant Washington. Instead they are thin and seem to hold the building down rather than support it. Gardens on the building platform, another Stone hallmark, surround the building. On the terrace side, tall wide windows alternate with equally tall and wide slabs of marble to take advantage of the river view. Stone hoped that the building would be "worthy of the great man for whom it has been named."[184] Critics, however, found it "bland and uninspiring,"[185] and "flat and lifeless."[186] Stone thought it represented "2,500 years of Western culture rather than twenty-five years of modern architecture."[187] Critics found it "totally lackluster, distrustful of creativity: the biggest box in the world [that] adds nothing to the art of architecture."[188]

Depending on one's appreciation of Stone's design style, McDonough Hall, completed the same year as the Kennedy Center, receives the same admiration and the same condemnation. Following the lessons of Wright, Stone sought to use the site to combine the advantages of an urban location with a college atmosphere. Unfortunately, the area was an urban wasteland rather than a vibrant urban landscape. Lucretia's Beauty Shop, Niosi's Grocery and Liquor Store, the Holmes Bakery, and most of the residents had departed the area. Creating a college atmosphere was equally daunting. Stone designed his four-story square building on his signature massive platform. (See photo on page 82.) To bring a campus ambiance, the podium was to be "liberally planted" with trees. The trees, however, were planted in boxes since there was no earth. The podium was so large it resembled a Roman forum more than a campus green. To understand its original enormity, one must visualize McDonough Hall without its later constructed East Wing, which sits on the west half of Stone's original podium facing its remnant. Moreover, the combination of the podium and the New Jersey Avenue stairway created a forbidding and foreboding entrance, hardly conducive to a social gathering or a welcoming invitation to enter. This entryway, then as now the Law Center's main entrance, did not serve that purpose until September, 2005.

Stone also used another of his signature elements, the overhanging flat roof; but it was stunted, offering neither shade nor breezeway to ward off the hot Washington sun. The facade contained alternating ground to roof rows of glass and masonry, again mimicking the Kennedy Center; but it was made from lesser material. Stone included a sunken courtyard on the lower level, now the covered lobby of the Hart Auditorium, but it was small, uninviting, and very hot in the afternoon sun.

The interior materials were more stark than the refined brick, glass, and paving stones that are visible on the outside. Moreover, budget shortfalls and disagreements with contractors provided less-than-masterful craftsmanship. The main floor walls were painted concrete block. Many of the walls remained uncovered block until the East Wing was built. But as Paul Dean noted at the

groundbreaking in 1968, "a building does not make a law building. A law school is produced by spiritual things. removes an obstacle to education and thought."[189] McD many of those obstacles. At the heart of the building, fro tions radiated, was a two-story library visible from a lar floor that was surrounded by classrooms. Approached b library housed an expanding collection of books and pr patrons. It originally occupied the current third McDonough.

The expanding and improving faculty finally had p for secretaries and research assistants, as well as f researchers. New classrooms and seminar rooms were av student groups had offices for their work. A multi-pu held almost 500 people. When McDonough Hall w Chief Justice Warren Burger, and counter-dedicated o law students and left-leaning lawyers and activists su Arthur Kinoy, Katie Rohrback, and Marion Barry, ever to a new phase of Georgetown's history.[190] Although cla were apparent, and though the nation was in turmoil the civil rights movement, it was clear to everyo Georgetown were over. New energy and purpose faculty alike.

In retrospect, the criticism of Stone and of his M changing understanding of architecture in Washingto pervasiveness of modern architecture in Washington ment was powerful and truly radical at the time McD In his Washington, D.C., buildings, Stone developed ernist architecture and set them down in a city domi Beaux Arts styles.

Today, the exterior of McDonough Hall seems w the addition of the East Wing. To many people, it is have seemed to its supporters when it was new. To i flaws as those in the Kennedy Center. The compar ings, however, should not be over-emphasized. Mc servative than the Kennedy Center, and has none often appear in Stone's work. McDonough is far m seems to convey its presence as an academic buildin the building's exterior expresses a pleasing sense of particularly beautiful. In fact, Stone's choice of b major influence on the selection of building mate buildings on the Law Center campus. Most recentl tects and the Whiting-Turner management team and mortar colors to ensure that the bricks of the ment those of McDonough Hall and the buildir

inspec
and F
integr
Th
idiom
dream
al style
to the
place f
archite
dream
new bι
our pu
borhoo

CLOCK TOWERS

MAY 27, 2004

As construction trailers begin to disappear, the installation of the interior elements of our buildings proceeds at a dizzying rate. Over one hundred workers are on the site almost every day installing drywall, millwork, lighting, and tile. The curved walls and domed ceiling that form the entrance to the Hotung Building have been framed. The glass railings and walls that surround the library entrance are being set. Carpet has been laid on the fourth floor and cherry millwork surrounds the elevator lobbies, bringing new hints of color to the Hotung Building. Cabinets have been hung in some of the library staff areas. Bookcases are being installed in faculty offices. One elevator is on line.

The terrazzo floor has been poured in the Sport and Fitness Center and grinders are bringing its multi-hued stone patterns to the surface. The walls of the basketball court and the intricate ceiling trusses have been painted. The branching outside trusses have been primed, and the columns are being wrapped. The pool has been tiled and grouted, showing off the racing lanes in blue and white. Tile on the pool deck and in the pool offices has also been set. Ceiling grids, coffers,[191] and lighting coves have been installed, suggesting the final appearances of some of the interior spaces. Fire alarm and security features are being mounted, air handling units are being tested, and kitchen equipment is arriving.

On the Tower Green, footings for the patio that surrounds the front of the Sport and Fitness Center are being poured. The most visible progress outside the buildings, however, is at the clock tower. All of the brick and precast concrete is in place. The GFRC (glass fiber reinforced concrete) cladding which will surround the clock face has been installed. The roof has been covered by its brilliant blue-green copper sheeting. Atop the tower rises a six-foot finial. Soon the clock itself will be mounted and the passing of time will be marked by chimes.

Time always intrigues. To Byron's Don Juan, "Time is, time was, time's past."[192] Augustine differentiated among three times: time past, time present, and time future.[193] To Einstein and to all of us in the modern world, time is no longer absolute. Unlike the ancients whose measure of time always seemed the same,

The Clock Tower on the Green
GEORGETOWN LAW CENTER ARCHIVE; SAM KITTNER, PHOTOGRAPHER

and barges."[176] He was fifty-two when he first considered himself wealthy and was sixty-six when his financial empire, the Marmac corporation of Parkersburg, West Virginia, was completed. He had boundless energy and a passion for work. "Business was both his work and his play."[177] "His mind was like a dynamo, powering a network of activities in dozens of places."[178] "He was tough, demanding, driving, intense, and impatient with inefficiency and insubordination;"[179] but he was loyal to people and to places that helped him along the way. McDonough had always been a contributor to Georgetown's alumni fund and had been a member of the Board of Regents. He was interested in the new building and told Dean that he wanted to do "something big." At a lunch at the Mayflower Hotel, McDonough offered Dean one million dollars for the Law Center's new building. At the time, it was the largest gift ever given to Georgetown. In return, the Board of Directors named the new building the Bernard P. McDonough Hall.

The architect Dean chose to design the building, Edward Durell Stone, was once described by *Time* magazine as "a pioneer modernist" and "one of the profession's freest spirits and by general consensus the most versatile designer and draftsman of his generation."[180] The passing of time has not been as generous to Stone's legacy as *Time* magazine was. Stone began his career as an apprentice for Coolidge, Shepley, Bulfinch, and Abbott, the firm started by H. H. Richardson and a forerunner of our current design firm. In the early 1930s, he started his own practice, designing residential buildings in the International Style,[181] an austere "modern" style of architecture featuring reinforced concrete, steel, glass block, and strip windows. This sleek, spare style abandoned ornamentation and lavish materials. By the 1950s, Stone had totally repudiated this modernist style, comparing it to "the latest model automobile, doomed to early obsolescence."[182] Following the lead of Frank Lloyd Wright, Stone began to see the importance of a building's site to the style of his architecture. His approach, still "modernist" but with more decorative elements, first appeared in hotel and academic architecture in the 1940s. It was decisively displayed in his stunning design of the U.S. Embassy in New Delhi. Its rectangular shape and temple-like form anticipated both the Kennedy Center and Georgetown's McDonough Hall.

Stone's work featured pierced screen walls, non-load bearing partitions behind structural members, overhanging canopies to provide shade and breezeways, and platforms that hid automobiles, created garden areas, and provided monumental settings. These stylistic elements appear in Stone buildings at Harvey Mudd College, the University of Chicago, the U.S. Naval Academy, and many other universities. Stone also employed these elements in many public buildings in cities around the country. In Washington, three Stone buildings bear these features: the National Geographic Society Building, the John F. Kennedy Center for the Performing Arts, and Georgetown's McDonough Hall.

Stone worked for more than eight years on the Kennedy Center, providing two concepts for the building. Unfortunately, the first and better design proved too costly.[183] The Kennedy Center we visit today is his second attempt to integrate the banks of the Potomac into the building's design. He emphasized the view of the Potomac, creating a grand foyer that simultaneously provides access to the three auditoria and to an equally grand terrace overlooking the river. Tall columns separated from the frame of the huge, rectangular, white marble building, support Stone's typical overhanging flat roof. These columns do not harken to the neoclassical columns of triumphant Washington. Instead they are thin and seem to hold the building down rather than support it. Gardens on the building platform, another Stone hallmark, surround the building. On the terrace side, tall wide windows alternate with equally tall and wide slabs of marble to take advantage of the river view. Stone hoped that the building would be "worthy of the great man for whom it has been named."[184] Critics, however, found it "bland and uninspiring,"[185] and "flat and lifeless."[186] Stone thought it represented "2,500 years of Western culture rather than twenty-five years of modern architecture."[187] Critics found it "totally lackluster, distrustful of creativity: the biggest box in the world [that] adds nothing to the art of architecture."[188]

Depending on one's appreciation of Stone's design style, McDonough Hall, completed the same year as the Kennedy Center, receives the same admiration and the same condemnation. Following the lessons of Wright, Stone sought to use the site to combine the advantages of an urban location with a college atmosphere. Unfortunately, the area was an urban wasteland rather than a vibrant urban landscape. Lucretia's Beauty Shop, Niosi's Grocery and Liquor Store, the Holmes Bakery, and most of the residents had departed the area. Creating a college atmosphere was equally daunting. Stone designed his four-story square building on his signature massive platform. (See photo on page 82.) To bring a campus ambiance, the podium was to be "liberally planted" with trees. The trees, however, were planted in boxes since there was no earth. The podium was so large it resembled a Roman forum more than a campus green. To understand its original enormity, one must visualize McDonough Hall without its later constructed East Wing, which sits on the west half of Stone's original podium facing its remnant. Moreover, the combination of the podium and the New Jersey Avenue stairway created a forbidding and foreboding entrance, hardly conducive to a social gathering or a welcoming invitation to enter. This entryway, then as now the Law Center's main entrance, did not serve that purpose until September, 2005.

Stone also used another of his signature elements, the overhanging flat roof; but it was stunted, offering neither shade nor breezeway to ward off the hot Washington sun. The facade contained alternating ground to roof rows of glass and masonry, again mimicking the Kennedy Center; but it was made from lesser material. Stone included a sunken courtyard on the lower level, now the covered lobby of the Hart Auditorium, but it was small, uninviting, and very hot in the afternoon sun.

The interior materials were more stark than the refined brick, glass, and paving stones that are visible on the outside. Moreover, budget shortfalls and disagreements with contractors provided less-than-masterful craftsmanship. The main floor walls were painted concrete block. Many of the walls remained uncovered block until the East Wing was built. But as Paul Dean noted at the groundbreaking in 1968, "a building does not make a law school, not even a new building. A law school is produced by spiritual things. A new building simply removes an obstacle to education and thought."[189] McDonough Hall removed many of those obstacles. At the heart of the building, from which all other functions radiated, was a two-story library visible from a large main hall on a lower floor that was surrounded by classrooms. Approached by a floating stairway, the library housed an expanding collection of books and provided seating for many patrons. It originally occupied the current third and fourth floors of McDonough.

The expanding and improving faculty finally had proper offices, with room for secretaries and research assistants, as well as for visiting faculty and researchers. New classrooms and seminar rooms were available. Law journals and student groups had offices for their work. A multi-purpose moot court room held almost 500 people. When McDonough Hall was dedicated in 1971 by Chief Justice Warren Burger, and counter-dedicated out in the street by radical law students and left-leaning lawyers and activists such as William Kunstler, Arthur Kinoy, Katie Rohrback, and Marion Barry, everyone was looking forward to a new phase of Georgetown's history.[190] Although clashing visions of education were apparent, and though the nation was in turmoil over the Vietnam War and the civil rights movement, it was clear to everyone that the old days at Georgetown were over. New energy and purpose prevailed in students and faculty alike.

In retrospect, the criticism of Stone and of his McDonough Hall reflected a changing understanding of architecture in Washington at that time. Despite the pervasiveness of modern architecture in Washington today, the modernist movement was powerful and truly radical at the time McDonough Hall was designed. In his Washington, D.C., buildings, Stone developed a romantic twist on modernist architecture and set them down in a city dominated by the Neoclassic and Beaux Arts styles.

Today, the exterior of McDonough Hall seems well-designed, especially after the addition of the East Wing. To many people, it is as attractive now as it must have seemed to its supporters when it was new. To its detractors, it has the same flaws as those in the Kennedy Center. The comparison between the two buildings, however, should not be over-emphasized. McDonough Hall is more conservative than the Kennedy Center, and has none of the structural tricks that often appear in Stone's work. McDonough is far more forthright and solid, and seems to convey its presence as an academic building. Though somewhat flawed, the building's exterior expresses a pleasing sense of rhythm. The glazed brick is particularly beautiful. In fact, Stone's choice of building materials has been a major influence on the selection of building materials for all of the subsequent buildings on the Law Center campus. Most recently, the Shepley Bulfinch architects and the Whiting-Turner management team spent many days testing brick and mortar colors to ensure that the bricks of the new buildings would complement those of McDonough Hall and the buildings that came after it. A close inspection will reveal that the bricks of McDonough, Gewirz, Hotung, and Sport and Fitness are all similar yet slightly different from one another, providing an integrated palette without being redundant.

The fusion of purpose and material, dreams and style, remains a powerful idiom in American education and architecture. Georgetown's campus began with dreams and a clearly defined purpose. It has been enhanced through architectural style and material. The architecture of each of the Law Center buildings speaks to the school's dreams and purpose. McDonough Hall brought a permanence of place for academic excellence in this neighborhood. It did so with a modernist architectural statement of power and forthrightness that embodied Paul Dean's dream of a modern Law Center, built on a bedrock of excellence and justice. Our new buildings continue that dream, in architectural styles that harken back to our purpose, but open us to an urban vibrancy that is returning to our neighborhood and to a community of nations of which we are an indivisible part.

XXII

CLOCK TOWERS

MAY 27, 2004

As construction trailers begin to disappear, the installation of the interior elements of our buildings proceeds at a dizzying rate. Over one hundred workers are on the site almost every day installing drywall, millwork, lighting, and tile. The curved walls and domed ceiling that form the entrance to the Hotung Building have been framed. The glass railings and walls that surround the library entrance are being set. Carpet has been laid on the fourth floor and cherry millwork surrounds the elevator lobbies, bringing new hints of color to the Hotung Building. Cabinets have been hung in some of the library staff areas. Bookcases are being installed in faculty offices. One elevator is on line.

The terrazzo floor has been poured in the Sport and Fitness Center and grinders are bringing its multi-hued stone patterns to the surface. The walls of the basketball court and the intricate ceiling trusses have been painted. The branching outside trusses have been primed, and the columns are being wrapped. The pool has been tiled and grouted, showing off the racing lanes in blue and white. Tile on the pool deck and in the pool offices has also been set. Ceiling grids, coffers,[191] and lighting coves have been installed, suggesting the final appearances of some of the interior spaces. Fire alarm and security features are being mounted, air handling units are being tested, and kitchen equipment is arriving.

On the Tower Green, footings for the patio that surrounds the front of the Sport and Fitness Center are being poured. The most visible progress outside the buildings, however, is at the clock tower. All of the brick and precast concrete is in place. The GFRC (glass fiber reinforced concrete) cladding which will surround the clock face has been installed. The roof has been covered by its brilliant blue-green copper sheeting. Atop the tower rises a six-foot finial. Soon the clock itself will be mounted and the passing of time will be marked by chimes.

Time always intrigues. To Byron's Don Juan, "Time is, time was, time's past."[192] Augustine differentiated among three times: time past, time present, and time future.[193] To Einstein and to all of us in the modern world, time is no longer absolute. Unlike the ancients whose measure of time always seemed the same,

The Clock Tower on the Green
GEORGETOWN LAW CENTER ARCHIVE; SAM KITTNER, PHOTOGRAPHER

scientists have revealed what poets always knew — that time flows are variable and elusive, dependent upon where one stands in the vast universe and on the speed, no matter how imperceptible, one travels.

Man's preoccupation with time began over 20,000 years ago. Archaeologists have found sticks and bones with scratched lines or carefully gouged holes that seem to be ancient calendars used to mark days between phases of the moon.[194] Five thousand years ago, Sumerians living in the Tigris-Euphrates valley developed a system that divided the year into thirty-day months and a twelve "hour" day.[195] Babylonians and Celts measured time 4,000 years ago with lunar cycles and star movements.[196] The Babylonian cycle was 364 days. The Egyptians, using Sirius or the Dog Star in the constellation of Canis Major, first measured the 365-day cycle in 4236 B.C.[197] Julius Caesar brought the 365-1/4-day calendar from Egypt to Rome.[198] The Julian calendar, however, proved slightly incorrect, and so it was modified by Pope Gregory XIII in 1582.[199] This is the calendar we use today.

All ancient civilizations of which we know sought to measure time to mark plantings and harvests, signal the commencement of war, and to honor their gods with celebration. The need to measure time, so elusive in the mind of a poet, remains a constant in the evolution of science, commerce, and philosophy. Measuring months and years did not suffice as human knowledge increased. Understanding ever smaller units of time preoccupied at least Western thought since the Middle Ages and continues to do so today.

True clockmaking began to appear in the Middle East and North Africa between 5,000 and 6,000 years ago.[200] Around 3500 B.C., Egyptians began to use obelisks to cast shadows that marked portions of the day.[201] As early as 1500 B.C., they used sundials to measure the passage of time. These horological instruments were not precise because of seasonal changes, but they served their agrarian populations and warring kings well enough. Merkhets measured "hours" at night by marking the movements of stars crossing a median.[202] Charts used to measure such movements are pictured in the tombs of Ramses VI and Ramses IX at Luxor, dating them to 1150 and 1120 B.C.[203] Amenhotep III owned water clocks, sometimes called clepsydrae[204] or "water thieves" in 1400 B.C., and the tomb of the craftsman Amenemhet suggests that he created water clocks with floating statues to mark the Egyptian hours as early as 1550 B.C.[205] Clepsydrae arrived in Greece by the fourth century B.C.[206] The great astronomical water clock of Su Sung stood in a thirty-seven-foot tower in the Chinese Emperor's court in 1088 A.D.[207] In 1126, it was carried away and destroyed by Chin invaders who could not make it work. Despite the Chinese preoccupation with calendars and astronomy, the clock then disappeared from China until the Jesuit Matteo Ricci reintroduced it to the Chinese court in 1605.[208]

The Egyptians' notion of a 24-variable-hour day and the sundial that measured it passed to Greece during the time of Alexander the Great and then to Rome about 293 B.C.[209] By 30 B.C., sundials were used throughout the "civilized" world.[210] They remained in use almost to the end of the Middle Ages.

Minutes, however, had no meaning to the ancients. Short intervals were often referred to with simile and metaphor such as "in the blink of the eye." Arabic astronomers may have been the first to use minutes, although the true source remains unknown. Minutes did not arrive in Europe, however, until the end of the Middle Ages.[211]

Early notions of time were far different from those of modern man. To the ancients, the notion of being "late" could only be determined by the rising and setting of the sun, the passage of water from a bowl, or the movement of the stars. Sometime between the thirteenth century and the sixteenth century, the need to understand ever-smaller units of time began to preoccupy Western thought. Time consciousness also began to change. Although sundials and water horologias measured time for monks and astronomers, time for common people was usually marked by periods of prayer, for example, matins, terce, and vespers. Indeed, our word *noon* comes from the None prayer period, which began shortly after the sun reached its peak. Bells usually tolled church time. Legend tells that church bells may have been invented in the Italian town of Nola in Compania, but that story may merely be a Latin play on words *(small bell)*.[212] Sabinianus is said to be the first Pope to order the ringing of church bells to signal the hours of the day. The practice expanded with the proliferation of church architecture during the Middle Ages. By the thirteenth century, church bells signaled the hour throughout all Christendom.[213]

During the course of the Middle Ages, the notions of Church time and secular time began to diverge as peasants moved to the cities and industry moved out of the monasteries. By the thirteenth century, clocks were in daily use. Like bells and relics, they were part of the church's and the monastery's ornamentation. Indeed, churches and monasteries competed with each other based on the grandeur of their clocks. Writers and artists were very conscious of time. Petrarch wrote about the "incalculable value of time."[214] Dante refers to clocks in the *Divine Comedy*.[215] Fourteenth-century art portrays various subjects in the presence of a sand hourglass, which replaced the small water clock during the late medieval period.

No one knows who invented the mechanical or wheeled clock, and historians can date it no better than the late thirteenth or early fourteenth century. Nor do we know whether the Europeans invented it or merely adopted it from China or the Arab world. One school of thought holds that the mechanical clock was merely a stepchild of other commonly used astronomical instruments. Galileo's need to measure velocity and acceleration led to an understanding of the uniformity of nature and of mechanical laws that made the prediction of astronomical events fairly accurate. His proofs, however, depended on the accurate measurement of time. The invention of the mechanical clock made Galileo's theories verifiable; but it did more than that. As described by Robert Andrew Millikan in 1932, these new scientific notions "transformed this world from one that is at bottom capricious and animistic, as was in fact both the ancient world and the medieval one, to a world that is dependable and in part, at least, knowable and controllable by man..."[216]

The essence of the mechanical clock was the verge and foliot escapement. This mechanism, consisting of an escape wheel and weights mounted on an axle, provided an oscillating movement that controlled the periodic movement of the hand on the clock. The speed of the wheel's movement was affected by adjusting the weights. These mechanical clocks were made of iron or, in the case of royalty, silver. Though they employed only an hour hand, they were more accurate and efficient than water clocks. Thus, mechanical clocks replaced large water clocks in Central Europe by the late thirteenth century. Water clocks completely disappeared from Europe by the end of the fourteenth century.[217]

Horological innovation continued throughout the Middle Ages. Clocks became portable when spring drives replaced weights at the end of the fifteenth century.[218] The minute hand was invented by Joost Bürgi in 1577.[219] Clocks became even more accurate when the pendulum, a timekeeping concept first noted by Galileo, was developed for a clock by astronomer Christiaan Huygens in 1657.[220] This mechanical innovation affected all manner of thought. Newton's postulates required accurate time measurements for their proofs. Descartes, Hobbes, and Kant all relied on time and on clock analogies as they expounded their philosophies. In time, even God was compared to a clockmaker.[221]

One of the first references to clock housings comes from Villard de Honnecourt in northern France.[222] His sketch, drawn in 1235 A.D., shows a wooden Gothic case with four floors and a gable. It claims to house a mechanical clock, but he drew no description. The relationship between bells, clocks, and towers spread during the late thirteenth century and thereafter. St. Paul's in London and the clock tower in Genoa were built in the mid-fourteenth century. Rouen had one in 1385. The oldest preserved clock tower, built in 1386, is at the Cathedral of Salisbury in England.[223] Artists depicted playable carillons in the early 1300s. Controlled by weights and pulleys and connected to the clock's escapement, these striking clocks were more far complicated than the clock itself. They became the pride of the emerging cities of Europe. Mechanical figures soon joined the bells atop the towers. Often accompanied by melodic chimes, these figures moved in and out of the tower as the clock stuck the hour. Moscow's first striking clock appeared in 1404, Dubrovnik's in 1389. The Cathedral at Norwich (1325) had a procession of monks. The three Magi walked around the tower of St. Jacques Hospital (1326) in Paris. An angel "flew" around St. Paul's. These astonishing inventions were intended to be more than mere entertainment. As Gerhard Dohrn-van Rossum reminds us, the cathedral protocol from 1407 in Chartre states that the "purpose of these contraptions was, right up to the nineteenth century ...to lure people into church, to astound them, and to strengthen the authority of the Church."[224]

In Milan (1322), Orvieto (1307), and Westminster (1369), clock towers were also used to strengthen the political control of their patrons and to regulate the ever-increasing mercantilism of the era. By the fifteenth century, life in the cities centered on their clock towers. Again in the words of Dohrn-van Rossum, "the striking clock was born in fact from the needs of urban life."[225] By the sixteenth century, even life in the villages and towns of the slightly backward German Empire kept tempo with the public clock. Clockmakers' guilds were formed in Paris in 1544, in Nuremberg in 1565, and in Geneva in 1601.[226] Bells had names, and chimes became recognizable and famous. The Westminster chime, probably composed by William Crotch or his master Reverend Joseph Jowett in the late 1700s, was based on a Handel aria.[227] Originally installed in the Cambridge tower, it was later used at Westminster and now carries that name.

Time had taken on a new meaning for Europeans, one that was far different from the world view of pre-mechanical man. Social complexity had arrived, and it was time-driven. In the words of Ben Franklin, "time was money."[228] By the early 1800s, 120,000 watches were being manufactured each year by 20,000 workers in Great Britain, a fact that escaped neither Adam Smith nor Karl Marx. Once "time" was reinvented, the need for greater accuracy produced better and better clocks and watches. In 1721, George Graham improved the pendulum clock's accuracy to an error margin of one second per day.[229] Today, simple quartz clocks with neither gears nor escapements provide anyone with amazingly accurate time measurement at little cost. Modern atomic clocks are now accurate to within one-millionth of a second per year.[230]

Clock towers, like fireplaces and academic robes, are no longer necessary in the modern world. Wrist chronometers, furnaces, and down jackets make them all unnecessary. Yet we continue to use them because they bring comfort and evoke traditions associated with human enlightenment and progress. Clock towers also bring a sense of place and purpose. Our tower has a traditional design reminiscent of clock towers on campuses around the western world. (See photo on page 90.) It reminds our neighbors that we are, at heart and purpose, a center of learning with roots that reach back to the first colleges of the Middle Ages. Nonetheless, our clock tower is distinctly modern as well. The movement of its clock is electronic rather than weight-driven; its settings are controlled by a GPS (global positioning derived from satellites) system. The tower employs no bell pullers; its chimes are programmed by computer. It will toll the familiar Westminster chime, but will also play a hundred other tunes at the turn of a switch. Like towers of old, it will combine invention and awe. As our tower signals the time to our community and to our neighborhood, it will mark not only the time of the poets and scientists, but also the time of the ancients who strove to understand their place in a vast universe where time has both relative meaning and no meaning at all.

XXIII

F STREET AND THE HIGHWAY TO NOWHERE

JULY 2, 2004

So many activities are occurring at the construction site that it is difficult to recount them all. New sidewalks have been set along First Street; concrete pavers are being set along F Street; and the alley behind the buildings is ready for repaving. New sewer lines are going in. Every day, another mechanical system or air handling system is being tested.

Inside the Sport and Fitness Center, floors have been laid in the aerobics rooms, the cardio and weight areas, and the spinning room. Glass walls are standing and the floors have been finished in the racquetball courts, anticipating the first serve. Concrete pavers now rest on the third-floor terrace, awaiting Adirondack furniture and weary athletes. Lockers have been installed on the first floor, and an intricate ceiling above the swimming pool will soon be visible. Fireplace boxes, metal column covers, and stone wall coverings are being installed on the second floor, completing the interior design of the cyber cafe, the juice and coffee bar, and the lounge area.

In the Hotung International Law Building, anigre millwork,[231] stone column covers, and custom shelving grace the library. Terrazzo risers are being set in the staircases. Lighting, wall paneling, desks, and blackboards give hints of the coming student-faculty discussions in the classrooms. Offices have carpets and bookshelves, data and electrical outlets. The moot court judges' bench, coffered ceiling, walls, and pilasters reflect the elegance of the United States Supreme Court, upon which our courtroom is modeled.

On the Tower Green, decorative louver grilles and an elegant Roman-numeraled clock face now command the Tower. Soon they will be joined by chimes to mark the passing of time. Landscaping preparation has begun on the Tower Green itself. Concrete sub-base has been poured for the Sport and Fitness terrace and the walkways. Soon their pavers will delineate the flow of pedestrians. Whiting-Turner construction trailers are being dismantled, a sure sign that the site is almost ready. Watering systems will soon be installed, followed by grass, trees, shrubs, and flowers that will add texture to the Tower Green. F Street as a thoroughfare will disappear, replaced by landscaping all the way to the north curb line.

According to the D.C. Historic Preservation Board, F Street ranks as one of the most important lettered streets in the original city plan drawn by Pierre L'Enfant.[232] Although L'Enfant sited most public buildings on the wider diagonal streets that were to be named for the states, F Street, NW, like 8th and G Streets, NW, served to connect the original Appropriations, that is, the lots on which major buildings, parks, and memorials were to be sited. As originally designed, F Street connected the Appropriation for the Executive Grounds (the President's House) with the Appropriation for the National Church (the idea of a National Church was later replaced by the Patent Office), and with the Appropriation for Judiciary Square. Moreover, L'Enfant used F Street as part of a Baroque triangulation device that reappears throughout his city plan. Instead of showing important vistas as "simple views down a street from one building to another,"[233] L'Enfant created oblique views of significant buildings and "an interlocking geometric composition" to display the grandeur of the city.[234] For example, when one looks at the Capitol while standing on Pennsylvania Avenue, one sees the building as it relates to the Mall (originally L'Enfant's Grand Avenue) even though the Mall itself is not visible. L'Enfant also wanted someone standing on F Street to see the National Church (or later the Patent Office) jutting out slightly into the street at the intersection of 8th Street to mark the cross-axis of his plan. As the cross-axis, 8th Street was placed midway between the President's House and the Congress House, and ran from the Potomac River, across the Mall, into the residential area of the City, and then out to the boundary of the Territory of Columbia. In addition, the Executive grounds were sited so that George Washington's successors could look down F Street from a window in the President's House and see clear across the Anacostia River.

The importance of F Street and its vistas to the L'Enfant plan notwithstanding, the street has suffered several indignities which contributed to our ability to close it to traffic. President Andrew Jackson initiated its spoliation. After the second Treasury Building burned down in 1833 (the first had also burned), Congress debated the site of the new building for three years. Unable to reach an agreement, they left the decision up to the President. According to a story that persists today, Jackson, in a pique, walked out of his office and planted his cane at a spot which would block his view of "the Capitol and its stiff-necked occupants."[235] He chose Robert Mills,[236] architect of the Patent Office and many other public buildings, to design the Treasury Building. Mills' magnificent neoclassical building, with its towering one-piece Ionic columns, succeeded in blocking Jackson's views of the Capitol. Sadly, it also blocked his view down F Street, compromising the original L'Enfant plan. Residents decried the destruction of the Pennsylvania Avenue vistas. Indeed, a movement began to destroy and relocate the Treasury Building. Mills and his defenders rallied in an attempt to save the building. In the end, the proposed cost of tearing it down and rebuilding it ultimately silenced the critics. Today, even though it stands in the middle of F Street, Mills' Treasury Building with its later additions remains one of the most admired public buildings in the Capital.

The U.S. Treasury Building designed by Robert Mills and Thomas U. Walter
LIBRARY OF CONGRESS, PRINTS AND PHOTOGRAPHS DIVISION

In the early 1900s, the F Street vista was again interrupted by the construction of Union Station. Given the importance of unifying the railroads into one station, and given the general decrepitness of the old Swampoodle neighborhood, there was no outcry when Daniel Burnham sited his beautiful Beaux Arts train station in the middle of F Street at First Street, NE. Although the building is clearly an architectural delight, the once-sweeping view along F Street to the Anacostia River was lost forever because of its siting.

The final depredation to L'Enfant's plan for F Street was the Center Leg Freeway, which runs in a ditch west of the Law Center. America's post-World War II love affair with the automobile coincided with or created a passion among American urban planners for highways. The District of Columbia was not immune. Despite the departure of many government employees who supported the war effort, the population of Washington had soared to over 900,000 by 1950.[237] In that same year, the population in the metropolitan area exceeded 1.5 million.[238] Although retailers saw their customers abandoning the inner city for the far reaches of the District and for the newly emerging suburbs, the demand

The Beaux Arts Union Station, designed by Daniel Burnham
LIBRARY OF CONGRESS, PRINTS AND PHOTOGRAPHS DIVISION

for downtown office space accelerated as trade associations, educational societies, and national planning groups recognized that the federal government was not about to give up its primacy in the affairs of the nation or the world. In 1950, there were over 600,000 civilian jobs in Washington, twice the number there had been in 1940.[239] Suburbanites driving into the city to work congested the streets, causing the police to complain that the overwhelming number of cars interfered with crime-fighting activities.

The National Capital Park and Planning Commission, authorized in 1945 by Congress to rebuild Washington's deteriorated neighborhoods, was beset by lobbyists from many special interest groups, each with a grand plan to end the blight and revitalize the city. Among the more powerful were the officials of the local departments of transportation and the sellers of beautiful and affordable automobiles who demanded that City transportation be improved. At first they were extremely successful. In 1947, the Whitehurst Freeway began to move commuters around the congested lower Georgetown area. In 1948, century-old elm trees were destroyed to build the Dupont Circle Underpass to ease automobile traffic and serve the city's busiest trolley line. The Capital Beltway, originally called the Circumferential Highway, was also designed in the mid-1950s. Its first segment, which included the Woodrow Wilson Bridge,[240] was completed in 1961. The entire sixty-four-mile highway was completed in 1964 at a cost of $190 million.[241]

The Center Leg Freeway was part of a larger project called the Inner Loop, which itself was part of an even larger scheme to reroute traffic along several corridors through the city and then out to the developing Capital Beltway. (See illustration on page 101.) The Inner Loop had several iterations. The South Leg was designed to run along the Potomac River, connecting the Southeast Freeway, the 14th Street Bridge, and the new Theodore Roosevelt Bridge before turning towards Georgetown, where it would connect with the Potomac River Expressway, a new highway to be paved over the C&O Canal. The last part of this plan was eliminated after Supreme Court Justice William O. Douglas challenged highway proponents to walk the entire length of the Canal with him to discover and then preserve its natural beauty. The East Leg was to have begun at the new Anacostia Freeway, cross the 11th Street bridge, and proceed along 11th Street near Lincoln Park to Florida Avenue. It would have destroyed a beautiful group of row houses on 11th Street built by Charles Gessford[242] between 1865 and 1867, now called Philadelphia Row. At Florida Avenue, the loop turned west and followed along T Street until it turned south above Dupont Circle to join up in lower Georgetown with the Potomac River Expressway. Another proposed highway, called the Northeast Freeway, would have commenced on the East Leg at Florida Avenue, and then continued along the railroad tracks to Silver Spring. Other features proposed at one time or another were a North Leg going up K Street from the East Leg to Georgetown, and a bridge over the Potomac River at the Three Sisters Islands. Planners also proposed an expressway along Missouri Avenue and another, called the Industrial Parkway, that would have run along New York Avenue and then to Baltimore via the new Baltimore Washington Parkway.

Fearful that the highways would diminish the grand views contemplated by L'Enfant, the planners intended to depress the highways below the surface of the city. The Mall would be spared by a tunnel running under the Lincoln Memorial. Each Leg of the Inner Loop would be built below the streetscape and bridged at strategic points. Remnants of the depressed highway system exist today at the E Street Expressway and at Virginia Avenue in Foggy Bottom, and at the Center Leg Freeway west of the Law Center. Obviously, such a system would have cut the city into several enclaves isolated by highways. Old Capitol Hill provides an example of how this plan would have degraded the city. The original Capitol Hill neighborhood began at the Navy Yard created on the Anacostia River by President John Adams and grew to the north. The Eastern Market, a Capitol Hill landmark located today at 7th and C Streets, SE, was originally sited at about 5th and K Streets, SE, between the Navy Yard and the emerging Capitol Hill commercial and residential neighborhood. Today, the Southeast Freeway, elevated rather than depressed, divides the Capitol Hill neighborhood at about Virginia Avenue, hampering efforts to unify and enhance the old 8th Street commercial district and the neighborhood south of the highway.

The Center Leg Freeway, approved in 1964, was also a companion of the urban renewal project developed for our East End and Northwest 1 neighborhoods in the 1950s. By the time it was completed in 1966, over four hundred dwellings had been demolished, displacing 1,600 people and more than one hundred businesses.[243] One of those buildings was the Standard Oil Company Building at the northeast corner of Constitution Avenue and 3rd Street, NW. Erected in 1931, it was commonly known as the Esso Building, and was reputed to be the largest and grandest service station in America. The building stood three hundred feet long and six stories high, and was clad in limestone. Given today's gas station architecture, it is difficult to comprehend the grandeur of this dignified neoclassical structure.[244] America's post-war love affair with the automobile carried over to the architecture of automobile showrooms and service stations. Early automobile service station design often included elements of Colonial, Georgian, Gothic, or other architectural motifs. None, however, surpassed the dignity of this building or its volume of business. The service station occupied the basement, first floor, and sixth floor of the building, moving cars between floors by elevator. Major businesses like Ford, Prudential, and the General Electric Credit Corporation leased space in the rest of the building, as did the Territory of Alaska and the United States District Court.[245] Like so many handsome residential and commercial buildings, the Esso Building could not hide from the "progress" of the 1950s and 1960s. The building was razed in 1964. It is commemorated in James M. Goode's *Capital Losses,* a book recounting the destruction of Washington's architectural treasures.

Several prominent churches along the proposed Center Leg route avoided the wrecking ball. All were spared after years of haggling with the government. The Center Leg was originally designed to follow a path between 2nd and 3rd Streets, a path that would have caused the demolition of four churches – Bible Way, Mt. Carmel, McKinley Baptist, and our neighbor, Holy Rosary. Fortunately for some of their congregations, Congressman Sam Rayburn thought the highway interchange at the Southeast Freeway was too close to the new House of Representatives office building that would one day bear his name. As such, the highway was rerouted in a way that brought it closer to 2nd Street, thus sparing the churches. Holy Rosary lost its rectory which was located at the rear of the church. In exchange, it was given the opportunity to build a new rectory in the middle of what used to be F Street, thereby again compromising the L'Enfant vista.

Notwithstanding the approval of the Center Leg Freeway, it was never completed. The portion of the Center Leg that was completed in 1973 ran a mere 1.4 miles from the Southeast Freeway interchange to Massachusetts Avenue.[246] It was twenty-two feet below sea level, with a tunnel under the Mall that ran 3,500 feet. The tunnel was sixty-six-feet wide from wall to wall and ran seven blocks of the sixteen-block highway. It had forty-one emergency phones, thirty cameras, sixty-four lane controls, 3,865 fluorescent lights, and twenty-eight fans to

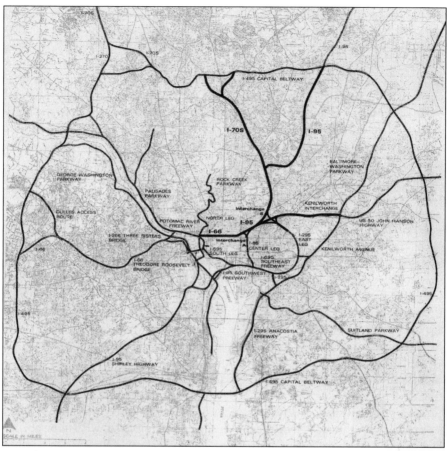

Map of the proposed Inner Loop highway system for Washington, D.C., circa 1960
MARTIN LUTHER KING, JR. MEMORIAL LIBRARY, WASHINGTON D.C., WASHINGTONIANA DIVISION

remove carbon monoxide from the tunnel. Costing $81 million, it was reputed to be the most expensive highway ever built at the time.[247] It was also the most technically complex. Despite its technological complexity, it became a highway to nowhere. Beyond Massachusetts Avenue, the highway became a pit that remained a parking lot until 1982, when it was extended to K Street, NW. The extension did nothing to change its fate.

Most of the Inner Loop plan was scrapped after years of controversy. Lawsuits by the Committee of 100, the D.C. Federation of Civic Associations, and other civic groups, protests by activists like Sammie Abbott and Peter Craig,[248] the demand for a new subway system, and the obvious racial discrimination associated with the plan ultimately resulted in its demise. Still, remnants remain. The Theodore Roosevelt Bridge, the Southeast Freeway, the Anacostia Freeway, and the depressed Virginia Avenue in Foggy Bottom are a few parts of the original plan that still exist. The road along the Potomac River and around the Lincoln Memorial that connects Independence Avenue with the Rock Creek Parkway and the E Street Expressway was built as a compromise. Old arguments about parts of the plan resurface from time to time. Debates continue about the existence of an interchange at Barney Circle on Pennsylvania Avenue, SE, and Virginia legislators still dream of a Three Sisters Bridge.[249] Nonetheless, the highway plan is dead. The intense and prolonged resistance to the Inner Loop ultimately saved the L'Enfant plan. Saving it turned out to be critical to the urban renaissance that we are experiencing in Washington today.

The history of local Washington is written on F Street. As conceived by L'Enfant, the street was a major design element for graceful living in the nation's capital. It was the center of an early residential area, populated by some of the most influential people of the newly founded republic. As the city grew after the Civil War, F Street became its most important commercial thoroughfare and the scene of fashionable balls attended by national and world leaders. When the city sought to redefine itself after World War II, F Street came to signify all that was wrong with that definition. Neighborhoods adjoining F Street suffered, while L'Enfant's plan was cast upon a scrap heap. Today, as the old downtown thrives anew, F Street has reawakened from its nightmare.

Little can be done now to fix the damage done to the L'Enfant Plan by the Center Leg Freeway. Plans to create housing or offices over the highway arise from time to time, but the money and the technology necessary to develop the site are elusive.[250] Our plan for F Street seeks to revive what is salvageable of L'Enfant's plan in the East End. The sight lines along F Street will remain open, leaving the vistas intact. Once the Tower Green is completed, we will be able to look east and see the grandeur of Burnham's Union Station. Our imagination can take us all the way to the Anacostia, the first great river of Washington, cleaner now because of the efforts of our own Institute For Public Representation. When we look west on F Street, Holy Rosary's Rectory will impede, but not obliterate, the view. We know that the axis at 8th Street, where the old Patent Building juts out, remains, and that the Treasury Building and the White House stand beyond. The Tower Green will complement a great center of learning, so necessary to L'Enfant's conception of a great city. The Tower itself will be the kind of public monument that he envisioned to liven the urban landscape, while the Green will bring the tranquility that he knew would be necessary in the capital of a great and busy nation.

Georgetown University was founded as our nation was born. The Law Center began as our nation redefined itself after a terrible Civil War. We are and always have been a part of this city, and it is part of us as well. No city planner on this continent ever conceived a more perfect urban design than Pierre L'Enfant. Our conception of the Tower Green and F Street pays homage to Pierre L'Enfant's vision, brilliance, and creativity, and is Georgetown's gift back to the city in which we live.

Construction on the Center Leg Freeway of the Inner Loop Highway System, circa late 1960s
WILLIAM BARRETT, COURTESY KIPLINGER WASHINGTON COLLECTION

The East Wing of McDonough Hall, designed by Hartman & Cox
GEORGETOWN LAW CENTER ARCHIVE; BILL GEIGER, PHOTOGRAPHER

XXIV

THE LAW CENTER EXPANSION YEARS

AUGUST 16, 2004

The final weeks of any construction project create tension, stress, and anxiety. Hundreds of details must be addressed. Tempers flare, voices are raised, and friendships begin to strain. Inspectors discover flaws where none were thought to exist and demand changes that delay the building's opening. Furniture installers wait at the lower floor hoping that inspectors will certify an elevator's operability. Inaccurate shop drawings show square columns where round ones exist, forcing slight relocations of furniture and the redrilling of the concrete floors for new electrical and data outlets. Ceiling designs become more difficult to install than originally anticipated, requiring hours of overtime. Future users of the buildings survey their spaces and find fault, forgetting that theirs is but one of hundreds of electrical outlets and dozens of bookcases that have been placed according to standard use patterns rather than individual preferences. Late deliveries bring complaints, ill will, and bad behavior from future users. They ignore the immense amount of coordination required to complete a $61 million project as they demand solutions for personal idiosyncracies.

Through it all, the work systematically continues. As the lighting and electrical contractors finish their work, Go Card swipes and closed circuit television (CCTV) cameras must be tied into the security system. After optical fiber is blown into the conduit, network engineers must install servers and tie in the data outlets so that telephones and computers work when the offices are occupied. Audiovisual engineers install and connect cable access television (CATV) systems, plasma screens, and televisions. Painters touch up previously painted walls and ceilings, while woodworkers erase nicks from anigre-paneled walls. Masons clean bricks and blocks and buff down rough edges on stone walls, while window-washers provide spotless views from the offices within. Fitness equipment arrives, the pool is filled, and mirrors and curtains are hung in the locker rooms, showers, and bathrooms. Basketball hoops are erected, the court is striped, and the glass walls of the racquetball courts are polished. The aerobic floors are redone because they do not meet our satisfaction. Crews scurry around daily, cleaning each area and recleaning as inspectors require additional work.

The Gewirz Residence, designed by Hartman & Cox
GEORGETOWN LAW CENTER ARCHIVE

Ceiling tiles are replaced as previously unnoticed leaks are repaired. Retail shelves are installed, kitchen equipment is tested, and stone for the fireplace is finally released by U.S. Customs. Damaged sprinkler heads are replaced just ahead of an inspector's visit.

Outside, pathway and sidewalk pavers are set and streetlights are installed. Landscapers set the grass pavers, fill them with soil, and then watch as hurricane-induced rains wash the topsoil away. This week we begin again, replacing the topsoil and adding sod to the surface of a simple yet clever planting system that will provide a beautiful lawn and yet be strong enough to support a moving fire engine. Dying trees are cut down as new trees and shrubs are planted. Watering systems are installed, and F Street is prepared for a new guard station and garage entry system.

All the while, the Georgetown Law/Whiting-Turner team perseveres, trapped between self-imposed deadlines and city inspection schedules. And then, on Friday the 13th, with the specter of hurricane winds and rain ahead of us, the final inspector releases his stickers and a certificate of occupancy is granted for the buildings. The Campus Completion Project, the culmination of almost 50 years of plans and dreams, is ready for occupancy.

Although the Campus Completion Project is nearing its end, one chapter remains to be told in the architectural history of the Law Center campus. McDonough Hall was barely completed in 1971 when growth and progress created new strains on the building. By 1977, the Law Center was seriously considering enlarging McDonough Hall, renting office space, and erecting another building. The library stacks were nearly filled, the building was crowded, and the space did not match the Law Center's ambition. In 1982, the Law Center's Planning Committee reported that the library in McDonough Hall exceeded its design capacity of 275,000 volume equivalents.[251] Twenty-five hundred students occupied the single building that served the Law Center's entire academic and administrative program.[252] Students were demanding even more services, more Law Journals, and more elective courses, all of which required more space. Since no Law Center housing existed, all students were commuters and campus life was nonexistent. In truth, the Law Center had no campus. Moreover, our neighborhood was virtually deserted and not very safe. Architectural critic Ben Forgey, when later recalling what the neighborhood around New Jersey Avenue and F Streets, NW, looked like in 1970, essentially said there was no there there.[253]

The full-time faculty was growing. In 1978, fifty-four full-time faculty taught at the Law Center. By 1984, the faculty was to grow to sixty-three, all of whom were expected to produce more scholarship, forge links with other scholars and policy analysts, and create institutes that would further the Law Center's goals for interdisciplinary learning. The growing Clinic Educational program was housed in rented space, some on the other side of G Street in the Levy Building, some downtown at 605 G Street, NW, and some at 25 E Street, NW. Classrooms for seminars and small sections were lacking since McDonough was designed with large lecture halls, the predominant venue for classroom instruction in most American law schools at that time.

In 1977, a committee appointed by Dean David McCarthy and chaired by Professor Frank Flegal began considering the challenges posed by the Law Center's ambitions in relation to its reality. Georgetown had purchased most of the few remaining houses and parcels of land on the Williams Library site. One of the buildings on the site, a restaurant called the Chancery, was once owned by a group of Georgetown faculty members. By then, however, it had become a topless bar whose owners held out until late in our planning process. At one point, the University's lawyer, Al Ledgard, reminded the bar owner that Georgetown had been in Washington for almost two hundred years and was likely to remain here for at least another two hundred. Citing the power of permanency, Al advised him that Georgetown would one day own his property, and would own it on our own terms. Because of the holdout, the original library plan was drawn to literally surround the restaurant. Over time, Georgetown sued the restaurant for operating a sexually-oriented business near a church (our chapel), the topless bar business declined, and the owner died. Georgetown then bought the property, and the southeast corner of the Williams Library was redesigned.

The Building Committee chose the firm of Hartman and Cox to design a building that could hold the library, the law journals, and the clinics. Established in 1965, Hartman and Cox had broken from the modernist trends of twentieth-century architecture and established a style that was contextual, that is, sensitive to a building's location and surroundings, and one which recalled the classicist school of architecture.[254] Hartman and Cox became leaders of the so-called "Washington School"[255] of architecture which was, in some sense, part of the postmodernist/contextual wave of architecture occurring in the 1970s. Old facades on Washington buildings began to be preserved as new construction rose behind them. Innovation in materials was explored. Architectural elements from older buildings were reassessed and reused with modern adaptation.

Warren Cox has stated that Washington is "more than a place; it is a state of mind."[256] Such thinking permeates his work and that of Mario Boiardi, a Hartman-Cox partner who helped design four projects for the Law Center. The Edward Bennett Williams Library is named for a legendary Washington lawyer and Law Center graduate. Williams was a first-class trial lawyer, counselor to famous and infamous clients, advisor to presidents, and a professor at Georgetown. After graduating from the Law Center in 1944, he went on to found Williams & Connolly, a prominent D.C. law firm. His clients included Senator Joseph McCarthy, former Secretary of Treasury John B. Connally, Teamster leader Jimmy Hoffa, and Frank Costello, the mobster upon whom the "Godfather" movies are based. The public initially did not know what to make of Williams since his clients included both Senator McCarthy and those who refused to answer questions regarding communist activities. His strong belief in the right to counsel for the accused and the competitive nature of criminal defense led him to take on some of the most difficult clients. Jimmy Hoffa, a

The Edward Bennett Williams Library, designed by Hartman & Cox
GEORGETOWN LAW CENTER ARCHIVE

Teamster leader whose body has never been found, once said, "Ed takes a case to win, not just for the fee." This competitive nature led Williams to roles as president of the Washington Redskins and owner of the Baltimore Orioles. After successfully arguing the first case before the Supreme Court concerning the application of the Fourth Amendment to electronic devices, he became the national expert on illegal wiretapping. As a public servant, Williams was twice appointed to the prestigious President's Foreign Intelligence Advisory Board and served as the treasurer for the Democratic Party National Committee. He also taught criminal law and torts at Georgetown from 1946 to 1956.

The Williams Library is a grand building in the Washington vernacular. Its rotunda and curved east end suggest the neoclassical buildings of the Federal Triangle, while its overall look has been called "greco-deco." Its three-story atrium with a central top-lit, interior court is reminiscent of the Corcoran Gallery. Its reading room recalls the Folger Shakespeare Library which Hartman and Cox remodeled between 1976 and 1983. Yet it is built in context with and sensitive to Edward Durell Stone's McDonough Hall. Like McDonough Hall, the Williams Library is placed on a podium and has a repetitive ordering of facades. It also emulates Stone's building in height. But it is not the same. Unlike McDonough Hall, it has no roof slab cornice. Three sides of the building are placed on the street line, whereas McDonough Hall sits entirely on the podium.

The Williams Library was one of the first Washington buildings to use decorative precast concrete, often mistaken for limestone, whereas Stone used brick and poured concrete for McDonough Hall. This combination of old and new, context and contrast, and invention and emulation can be seen in Hartman-Cox buildings throughout the city. The Sumner School complex, the building at 1001 Pennsylvania Avenue, Market Square, and others all incorporate the Hartman-Cox design philosophy.

The $25 million Williams Library, completed in 1989 under the leadership of Dean Robert Pitofsky, was to be only the first of the Hartman-Cox projects at the Law Center. During the course of the library project, the original plans were changed. The later Boiardi and Cox design moved the clinics and a new cafeteria into an underground expansion to the west side of McDonough Hall. Renovations to the old library spaces on the third and fourth floor of the building avoided the labyrinthian passages of the original design and brought light to the building's interior. Many of the interior concrete block walls were covered over, painted, and decorated to eliminate the industrial feeling that permeated the building.

In the 1980s, Georgetown partnered with the Tobishima Company of Japan to co-develop the parcel of land south of the Law Center. A little fish restaurant and the Salvation Army offices and bookstore made way for a project that envisioned Georgetown building a residence hall on the west side of the site and Tobishima erecting a $150 million office building on the east side. A shared urban park would have joined the two buildings. The vagaries of the Japanese economy, however, ended Tobishima's plans for its flagship American development, and eventually caused the demise of Tobishima itself. Georgetown, however, continued to move forward.

The $23 million Bernard and Sarah Gewirz Residence Hall, named for a local developer and philanthropist who attended Georgetown Law Center and his wife, was completed in 1993 under the leadership of Dean Judith Areen. Warren Cox and Mario Boiardi again combined context and contrast when designing a twelve-story residence hall that had a childcare center and fitness rooms below grade and a ceremonial ball room and balcony at the top. (See photo on page 106.) Interior and exterior columns and pilasters reflect the grandeur of Washington. A series of projections and recessions create a rhythm on the long east and west facades. The decorative Union Jack railings, pilasters, and half columns distinguish the building from the mundane and suggest a first-class apartment building. According to critic Ben Forgey, "playful little triglyphs … [on the curtain wall] are a sign of the design's distinct origins in the classical Doric order."[257] The building, however, remains contextual. The cylindrical drum rising from the fifth to the eleventh floor echoes the rotunda of the Williams Library, while the fourth-floor cornice over the door denotes the lower heights of the other Law Center buildings. Repetitive ordering of the facades recall both McDonough Hall and the Williams Library, and the arcades on all three buildings unite them. The brick color resembles, but is not identical to, the color of McDonough Hall, while precast cornices and lintels recall the Williams Library. Again, according to Forgey, it is "a quietly distinguished building, that literally and figuratively, helps to transform the things around it."[258] Finally, the arch over the door connects the building to Georgetown's history. Its shape resembles the entry arch at the Law Center's prior building at 5th and E Streets, NW, built by James Denson. That arch now decorates a wall at the east end of the Library Quad.

The last project Hartman-Cox designed for the Law Center was the East Wing of McDonough Hall. (See photo on page 108.) Completed in 1997 under the leadership of Dean Judith Areen, the East Wing houses classrooms, offices, and conference rooms. Built at a cost of $12 million, the new wing improves the east facade of McDonough Hall without looking like a last-minute fix. Stone's unwieldy podium is shortened, thus making it more inviting. The color of the bricks is identical but their shape is slightly concave, bringing "new interest" to the curtain walls. The wing's height lines up with McDonough Hall and retains Stone's signature flat protruding eave. The rotunda and precast concrete recall the Williams Library and the Gewirz Center. The architects reproduced Stone's vertical piers and windows but introduced architectural hierarchy to the facade. In addition, the piers are fluted rather than flat. In sum, like all Hartman-Cox/Boiardi projects, the East Wing is contextual but contrasts with and improves on the original.

The engineering for the East Wing is equally impressive. Because it is built over the Philip Hart Auditorium, essentially a large cavern incapable of holding the weight of a building, the wing had to be hung over rather than set on the surface. Mining equipment was brought into the McDonough Hall garage to dig holes fifty feet deep beneath the garage floor, in which supports were set to hang the building. Hartman and Cox had performed a similar feat when remodeling the Folger Library.[259] In both cases, the architects provided a sophisticated solution to a complicated engineering problem.

The concepts of context and innovation and the blend of old and new architectural elements introduced by Hartman-Cox and Boiardi resonated in our planning for the Hotung Building and the Sport and Fitness Center. Architects from Shepley Bulfinch Richardson and Abbott and from Ellerbe and Becket studied our campus and borrowed design elements from the earlier buildings. They have created two striking architectural ensembles that break from earlier motifs while respecting their integrity. Both new buildings recall elements of earlier Law Center buildings and treat them with respect without replicating their essential nature. As we begin to occupy the new buildings this week, their design reminds us of both our venerable past and our limitless future.

The Georgetown Sport and Fitness Center, designed by Shepley Bulfinch Richardson and Abbott
GEORGETOWN LAW CENTER ARCHIVE; HOLLY EATON, PHOTOGRAPHER

THE GEORGETOWN SPORT AND FITNESS CENTER

SEPTEMBER 9, 2004

Tomorrow we celebrate the opening of the Georgetown University Law Center Sport and Fitness facility. Designed by Shepley Bulfinch Richardson and Abbott, with the assistance of Ellerbe Becket and Group Goetz, this stunning athletic center with its welcoming Tower Green has transformed both the Law Center and our old East End neighborhood. The architectural goals for the site were to develop a formal, urban architectural experience that strengthened the existing character of the campus and to provide a sequence and variety of spaces using form, mass, and materials that complemented and completed the existing buildings on the Law Center campus. Our goals have been met. The arrangement and design of the new buildings complete the evolution of the campus as an urban academic center, strengthen its sense of identity, and provide that variety of activities and experiences that are consistent with the Jesuit tradition of *cura personalis*,[260] that is, caring for the whole person.

The 60,000-square-foot Sport and Fitness Center is contextual, and thus, its detailing and scale reflect the other buildings on the campus. Its height is approximately the same as McDonough Hall and the Williams Library. Its brick color blends with that of McDonough Hall and the Gewirz Residence, yet it is not identical. There is a range of brick colors that add subtle variations and a vitality to the walls. As in other buildings on campus, the Sport and Fitness Center has architectural reveals[261] set in the masonry to break the plane of the large wall surfaces, making them more human in scale. Set back between the more formal Hotung International Law Building and Gewirz Residence Hall, the Sport and Fitness Center uses its great expanse of glass to welcome and protect its visitors. Indeed, the building is open and transparent at all levels to clearly indicate its informal functions and to permit patrons to see in and out. Its north facade celebrates this principle with a four-story glass curtain wall, articulated by four elegant branching columns that reach the roof. The support for the roof, also visible from both the inside and the outside, is an intricate system of trusses that is as much a piece of art as it is a roof support.

The non-academic character of the Sport and Fitness Center is reflected in a physical presence that is different from its companion and from the other campus buildings. Though physically connected to the Gewirz Residence and to Hotung, the Sport and Fitness Center is designed to function differently from its neighbors. As one enters the Sport and Fitness Center, there is no doubt about its separate design and purpose. The cafe and dining spaces on the second floor display a modern, almost European design that is at once playful and relaxed, but strong and sleek. The upper and lower floors clearly define the building's character as a recreation center.

The building's playful purpose surrounds patrons as they enter the second floor from the Tower Green. Once inside, they may choose to dine at the Courtside Cafe, purchase items from the Recess Express, or choose from a wide array of athletic activities. A two-story-high atrium lounge, two fireplaces, and a double-pool fountain signal areas for quiet thought and conversation in a building designed primarily for active enjoyment. The Recess Express will supply the retail needs of both Fitness Center visitors and Gewirz residents. The cafe, serving traditional student fare, overlooks the lap pool to the south and the Tower Green to the north. A juice and coffee bar, also serving wine and beer in the evening, adds to the casual nature of the room. Both modern dining furniture as well as comfortable, casual chairs and sofas are available for more relaxed camaraderie. The Courtside Cafe and lounge, like the entire campus, has wireless internet connectivity so that patrons can access legal research and web-based course materials, read their e-mail, and peruse their student accounts while they eat, play, study, or relax.

Those choosing to exercise will register at the desk opposite the main door. There they will be directed to the locker rooms and pool below, or to the sports equipment desk, exercise rooms, and game courts above. The four-lane, twenty-five-meter lap pool on the first floor is in a naturally lit, high-ceilinged space with windows that open above to the dining area on the north and to the exterior on the south. One hundred and fifty day lockers and a whirlpool are located in each locker room. Staff offices, a towel service and laundry, massage rooms, and rooms for health and fitness counseling are also located on the first floor.

The third floor of the Sport and Fitness Center contains a weight training and exercise room overlooking the atrium and the Green. Over sixty pieces of equipment, some with computer, video, and audio enhancements, are available to achieve one's fitness goals. There are thirty-two separate cardio machines, three Nautilus chest machines, three Cybex and three Nautilus back machines, three Nautilus shoulder machines, two Nautilus arm machines, five Nautilus and two Cybex leg machines, two Nautilus abdominal machines, and five Nautilus XPlode machines for a complete circuit training experience. Many of the treadmills overlook the Tower Green and McDonough Hall. In addition, there is an assortment of free weights, presses, benches, and crossovers to turn anyone into Arnold Schwarzenegger. Two aerobics rooms and a spinning room with twenty-eight bikes are located to the south side of the third floor. Those unsure of their physical capacity may employ personal trainers for a fee.

The fourth floor contains two glass-backed racquetball courts and a double-height, maple-floored basketball court that converts into two volleyball courts or two basketball half-courts for intramural competition. The Tower Green is visible from the courts through tall glass windows. Classes in dance, racquetball, cardio, kickboxing, spinning, pilates, self-defense, yoga, swimming, BOSU, and sports conditioning will be available. When the workout is over, patrons will cool down in Adirondack deck chairs on a fourth-floor balcony overlooking the Tower Green.

The stone plaza in front of the Sport and Fitness Center and the Tower Green are designed to be experienced by passersby as well as users. They serve to connect McDonough Hall to the Sport and Fitness Center and to the Hotung Building and provide a grand entrance to the new buildings. The entrance to Sport and Fitness relates to the McDonough Hall entrances and to the pedestrian routes through the campus. Moreover, the combination of the Green, the plaza, and the glass curtain wall create an inside/outside experience that enlivens the area and makes it feel safe and pleasant. This inside/outside experience is further enhanced because the plaza's fan-shape design mimics the curve of the building's facade. The pattern of the plaza's stone pavers also reflects the deliberately off-center orientation of the interior floors and walls. They also resemble the pattern of the cafe's terrazzo floors. Stone benches on the plaza, the soon-to-be-added tables and chairs, and the glass curtain wall reinforce the integrated indoor/outdoor experience whether one is dining, studying, or engaging in conversation.

The edge of the stone plaza flows seamlessly into the Tower Green. The main area of the Green follows the natural downward slope of the land between 2nd and 1st Streets. Despite this eastern-sloping grade, the Green is flat enough to allow an impromptu touch football game in the fall or a frisbee tournament in the spring. Trees and shrubs are modest to allow for such activities; yet when the trees mature and additional benches are placed, there will be ample quiet areas for dreaming and contemplating one's future and past.

Rising above the Tower Green is our elegant brick and precast campanile, topped by a copper roof. Though built in context, it is a structure unto itself. It commands attention from both inside and outside the campus, yet does so with grace and charm. It reflects our past, but also suggests our permanence. Tomorrow the clock will begin to mark the flow of our lives, pleasantly chiming the hour to add to the ambiance, and reminding our neighbors that we are a place of academic reflection and a potent partner in the future of our city and our world.

None of this would have been possible without the vision of former Dean Judith Areen and the generosity of Dallas business leader and 1978 Law Center graduate Scott K. Ginsburg. As a child in Sioux City, Iowa, Ginsburg was fascinated with television cameras and courtroom lawyers, two interests he has retained throughout his life. After graduation, he served as Staff Director for the Senate Subcommittee on Employment, Poverty, and Migratory Labor and the Senate Subcommittee on Social Security. He also worked on several Senatorial campaigns, including that of former Senator John Culver of Iowa, before moving to Dallas to embark on a career in media ownership. Ginsburg was the founder of Evergreen Media Corp., Statewide Broadcasting, Inc., and H&G Communications, Inc. He is currently chairman of Digital Generation Systems. His cumulative experiences in law, politics, business, and philanthropy have been the foundation for a string of notable achievements in both the Dallas and Georgetown communities.

Athletics have always been an important part of Ginsburg's life. Remembering his own experiences at the Law Center, he wanted to contribute to the quality of the Georgetown students' lives. He hopes his gift will remind our community that "recreation and fitness are important parts of law school life, and that it will inspire other alumni to support the Center's facilities."

The partnership of Mr. Ginsburg and Dean Areen have produced an extraordinary Sport and Fitness Center. No free-standing law school in America, and few university-based law schools, provide a recreation center as magnificent as ours. A hundred years ago, a thriving neighborhood with homes, churches, and businesses occupied this site. A mere three years ago, nothing remained but a parking lot and the Tobishima Company's shattered dreams of a flagship commercial property. Today, the Georgetown Sport and Fitness Center and its companion, the Hotung International Law Building, form a quadrangle with McDonough Hall and the Gewirz Residence Hall that will bring new activity, new conversation, and new academic inquiry to our community. The neighborhood will once more reverberate with energy, laughter, and purpose. Vitality and vibrancy, silenced for so many years, has finally returned to the old East End neighborhood.

THE ERIC E. HOTUNG
INTERNATIONAL LAW BUILDING

OCTOBER 26, 2004

Tomorrow, we celebrate the opening of the Eric E. Hotung International Law Building. In doing so, the Georgetown Law Center completes a saga of academic excellence that is intertwined with the history of the Federal City. The Law Center began its educational mission in 1870 in a few simple rooms at the corner of 4½ Street and Pennsylvania Avenue, NW. During the ensuing years, it maintained a peripatetic existence throughout downtown Washington, occupying buildings on five sites before it settled at New Jersey Avenue and F Street, NW. At various times in its history, the Law Center's stability, too often fragile, was tested; but on each occasion, its dreams were maintained and it emerged stronger than before. Today, it is a giant among academic institutions. Its faculty includes some of the best legal scholars and teachers in academia; its students are among the most talented law students in the nation; its programs in clinical education, international law, and constitutional law are models for other schools to emulate. Now, after 134 years, it has a campus that retains its historic ties to the National City and is the equal of its academic aspirations.

It is fitting that we complete this project this year. Fifty years ago, Paul Regis Dean became Georgetown's dean. Often called the father of the modern Law Center, Dean initiated its march to academic greatness and foresaw its future emerging in the old East End neighborhood. So as we celebrate the generosity of Eric Hotung, we also celebrate the vision of Paul Dean and the deans who followed him: Adrian Fisher (1969 - 1975); David McCarthy (1975 - 1983); Robert Pitofsky (1983 - 1989); and Judith Areen (1989 - 2004). Each was the perfect choice for the time, and each contributed to the Georgetown we know today. As we begin a new era under the leadership of Dean Alex Aleinikoff, the story will continue with new vision, new directions, and new accomplishments.

It is also fitting that the Law Center's newest building is dedicated to international, comparative, and transnational law. From its birth, Georgetown has welcomed students from foreign countries. Joseph I. Rodriguez, a resident of Cuba, was a member of the Law Center's first class in 1870.[262] Today, nearly three

The Eric E. Hotung International Law Building, designed by Shepley Bulfinch Richardson and Abbott
GEORGETOWN LAW CENTER ARCHIVE; HOLLY EATON, PHOTOGRAPHER

hundred students from sixty-four[263] different countries are enrolled, comprising 12% of the student body. The design and construction process of the Hotung Building reflected this multicultural experience. It was designed and built by workers whose presence in America began with a migration from one of thirty-six separate nations located on six different continents.

The Hotung International Law Building was designed by Ralph Jackson, a partner at the architectural firm of Shepley Bulfinch Richardson and Abbott. Shepley Bulfinch was founded in 1874, just four years after the Law Center's birth. One of the oldest architectural firms in the country, Shepley Bulfinch has designed buildings that are among the most admired in America. Trinity Church and the Ames Building in Boston, the Art Institute and the old Public Library in Chicago, the Allegheny County Courthouse in Pittsburgh, Stanford University, and Harvard Medical School all reveal a vision of design excellence that has permeated the firm since its founding. Indeed, it is not an exaggeration to say that the civic fabric of both Chicago and Boston owes much to the talent within this firm.

The very names of the firm's partners give insight into the history of American architecture. Henry Hobson Richardson gave his name to a distinctly

American style of architecture that "adapted historical European architectural forms to newly emerging American needs."[264] Called Richardson Romanesque, the style was emulated throughout the country. Georgetown's prior home at 506 E Street, NW, paid tribute to this style. Richardson's influence extended beyond his life. New York architects Charles McKim and Stanford White trained in his studio. Chicago architects Louis Sullivan and Frank Lloyd Wright were influenced by his work. Frederick Law Olmsted, the designer of the Capitol grounds, was a frequent collaborator. Edward Durell Stone, architect of McDonough Hall, studied there as well. Partner Francis Bulfinch is also well-known and admired, especially by those who treasure American buildings that are closely related to the nation's history. He designed the Massachusetts State House and the Maine State House, and his renovation of Faneuil Hall gave us the building that we know today. The Shepleys, father and son, and Abbott, were not as renowned as Richardson or Bulfinch. Nonetheless, they also contributed to the firm's reputation for design and engineering excellence.[265]

The passage of time has not diminished the firm's skills or influence. Subsequent generations of Shepley Bulfinch architects maintained its tradition of excellence in buildings created for Vanderbilt Medical School, Northeastern University, Brown, Wellesley, Cornell, and others. In the words of Vincent Scully, Sterling Professor Emeritus of Art History at Yale, the firm has "moved seamlessly from the late nineteenth century into the present."[266] These traditions of excellence and civic virtue continue today as a new century dawns. A new generation of architects at Shepley Bulfinch have redesigned an academic campus for a new generation of lawyers studying at Georgetown Law Center.

The International Law Building is named for Ambassador Eric E. Hotung, CBE,[267] a world-renowned philanthropist and financier. Born in Hong Kong in 1926 and raised in Shanghai, he is the eldest grandson of Sir Robert Hotung — the last of Hong Kong's Merchant Princes and a prominent leader in the Chinese community. Ambassador Hotung came to the United States in 1947 and graduated from Georgetown University in 1951. Following the passing of his grandfather and father in the late 1950s, he returned to Hong Kong to direct his family's affairs. Ambassador Hotung's humanitarian work has taken many forms and has touched the lives of people in need throughout the world. During the 1950s and 1960s, he provided low-cost housing to the thousands of displaced Chinese refugees who came to Hong Kong seeking shelter. In 1965, he founded the Eric Hotung Trust Fund to improve education in Hong Kong and to encourage young people to study abroad. During the 1970s Ambassador Hotung labored to create better relations between China and the United States. By organizing delegations to travel back and forth between the two countries, he helped arrange avenues of diplomatic communication that fostered a heightened level of mutual understanding and purpose between these two powerful cultures.

Ambassador Hotung remains deeply invested in China's development and social welfare. He is a director of the Soong Qing Ling Foundation for Children and created a fund in Guangxi to teach safer childbirth practices, thereby significantly reducing the mortality rate of women and children in the region. Perhaps his greatest humanitarian achievement occurred in the nation of East Timor. In 1999, after learning about the plight of the East Timorese people following their newfound independence, he arranged the successful transportation of over 12,000 refugees from West Timor to East Timor by purchasing a vessel and supporting its operation for a two-year period. He also established free health clinics that have benefitted countless Timorese people. His dedication to the Timorese people and the newly forged nation of East Timor continues to this day, as he serves as Ambassador at Large and Economics Advisor for Timor-Leste. No building dedicated to transnational and international law and understanding could be more appropriately named.

The challenge facing the architects of the Hotung Building was to create a dramatic academic building in a traditional campus vernacular, while simultaneously creating a bold and modern architecture ensemble that opened the campus to the city and the world. To quote principal architect Ralph Jackson, Georgetown needed a building that exuded "restrained elegance."[268] He saw Georgetown at this moment in its history as wanting to proclaim its intention to pursue global academic excellence, but not wanting to appear aloof. He saw a school needing to nurture its own academic life, "but also wanting to contribute to life along the street — to be part of the neighborhood, and indeed the world."

The Hotung Building succeeds dramatically. Again quoting Jackson, the Hotung Building is a statement about "civility and urbanity" reminiscent of other grand Washington buildings. It communicates the notion that the building is "about people, democracy, and accessibility" and not about the "sometimes rigid strictures of academic hierarchy." Like its companion, the Sport and Fitness Center, the Hotung Building is contextual. It reflects the existing palette of textures and colors that distinguish the Law Center buildings from others in the neighborhood. Existing campus cornice lines, podiums, and floor levels are key to the Hotung Building design. The building is similar in scale and exhibits the same quality of detail that is evident in the Williams Library and McDonough Hall. Although the inspiration for the Hotung Building's form, material, and detail is drawn from existing campus buildings, Hotung is clearly different from its predecessors. Unlike McDonough Hall, the Williams Library, and the Gewirz Residence Hall, the Hotung Building entrances are off-center. Its cornice is bolder and suggests an Eastern rather than Occidental antecedent. The public's first view of each of the Law Center's buildings suggests its different function and marks a different period of time in the Law Center's East End sojourn. McDonough Hall, the Williams Library, and the Gewirz Residence Hall all look inward to our own community. Each presents a formal academic appearance and suggests a function that is protective and somewhat isolated from the surrounding neighborhood. The Sport and Fitness Center, while presenting a more casual approach to campus life, is sited in a way that also keeps it insulated from the outside world. The Hotung Building, however, has dual purposes. It presents a formal face that opens up to the city on the east and a somewhat softer campus orientation to the west. Although its rigorous and formal arrangement of windows and cornices suggest the rigorous and austere nature of the law, its windows are large and the glass is clear to connote the transparency and accessibility of the law and learning in America. The step pattern of the fenestration proclaims an elegant urban building that is part of the city and the world. Nonetheless, the Hotung Building retains the feel of an academic center, especially when viewed from the Tower Green.

The interior finishes of the 120,000-square-foot building suggest the formality of international organizations along with the traditions of academia. Cherry anigre walls surround the second floor, the elevator lobbies, and the John Wolff International and Comparative Law Library, providing a rich and stately sense of place. The furniture in the lobby is formal though comfortable, encouraging study and diplomatic conversation. The Wolff Library is the central feature of the Hotung International Law Building. It occupies the third and fourth floor of the Hotung Building and contains 103,250 volumes and volume-equivalents. The tables and carrels are gracefully designed and possess a dignified and cultured style that blends harmoniously with the architecture. Visiting international scholars and student study groups will find five scholar studies, eight scholar carrels, and four group study rooms available for their use. This comfortable setting accommodates the research efforts of two hundred patrons at one time. Reference and circulation desks, online search stations, a computer training laboratory, and administrative offices for the International Law Librarian and her staff support the work of these students and scholars.

Professor John Wolff, for whom the library is named, served the Georgetown community from 1961 to 2005. For forty-four years, he taught numerous courses in international and comparative law in both the J.D. and the LL.M. programs. In addition, he published many articles in numerous American and German legal publications. Professor Wolff graduated with a LL.D. from the University of Heidelberg and later received his LL.M. from Columbia University. In his long and illustrious career, he served as a lieutenant colonel in the Army Judge Advocate General's Corps, as a deputy to the U.S. representative to the United Nations War Crimes Commission, as an advisor to the U.S. Department of Justice on issues of international and foreign law, and as the deputy chairman of the Federal Bar Association's Council on International Law. Professor Wolff also lectured at the universities of Munich and Muenster and at the Law Society of Berlin. Through his ninety-ninth year, he continued to teach International and Comparative Law to grateful students at the Georgetown Law Center. He missed his his final day of class in the fall semester of 2005 and died shortly thereafter. Nonetheless, his final exam was ready and given to his students.

Changes in the way legal education is delivered and the growth of the scholarly and teaching activities of the Georgetown faculty guided Shepley's interior design of the Hotung Building's twelve new classrooms. State-of-the-art medium-sized classrooms are located on each of the first and second floors. They are horseshoe-shaped to encourage serious conversation and debate. Their modern and varied lighting patterns visually suggest the energy that we expect from the discussions that occur within the rooms. A smart-podium with touch-screen controls enables faculty members to integrate online and audiovisual materials into their teaching. Professors can introduce physical evidence and printed documents to the class using high-definition evidence presenters. A sophisticated sound system and optimized room acoustics create an ideal environment for class discussions. An advanced fiber-optic-cable-infrastructure combines with wireless connectivity to allow students to tap into internet resources while in class.

In addition to the two larger classrooms, nine new combination seminar/conference rooms are placed throughout the building. These rooms are equipped with an advanced infrastructure for audio and video recording, webcasting, and videoconferencing. Large monitors can be used to display audiovisual materials. As they can in the larger classrooms, students in the seminar rooms are able to connect wirelessly to the internet. These smaller classrooms permit students to apply the theory they have learned through traditional lecture methods by engaging in simulated litigation exercises, small group discussions, and collaborative problem-solving.

The Supreme Court Institute Moot Courtroom is located on the second floor. More than 60% of all United States Supreme Court cases are now mooted at Georgetown's Supreme Court Institute. To better prepare the advocates, the Moot Court is designed to evoke the interior of Supreme Court courtroom. Though not an exact replica, it provides advocates the opportunity for a dress rehearsal in an environment strongly resembling the actual Supreme Court chamber. The wood finishes, the leather furniture, and the design and color of the carpet are strikingly similar to that of the real Court chamber. Doric pilasters line the walls in a manner reminiscent of the Supreme Court's imposing marble Ionic columns. Round ceiling light fixtures set within coffers suggest the medallions in the Court's coffered ceiling, while molded elliptical designs on the face of the Moot Court bench and rail are reminiscent of circular patterns on those of the Supreme Court.

One of the more unusual characteristics of the Supreme Court is the intimate nature of the Court chamber. Advocates stand in close proximity to the nine Justices and the Court's well seems small in comparison to the building's imposing facade and public halls. Our designers replicated the unique spatial relationship between the litigant's podium and the Justices' bench to help lawyers gain comfort with the intimate yet overpowering nature of the Court. The shape of the bench and its proximity to the advocate's podium reproduce the tension of an actual argument. White and red lights on the lectern warn of, and then command, the end of each argument just as they do in the Supreme Court. Red curtains and an ornate clock, which paradoxically is not to be watched by advocates during an oral argument, hang behind the bench, adding yet another touch of reality to the rehearsal experience.

Because the Moot Court will also serve the needs of our trial advocacy program, it can be quickly transformed from an appellate court to a trial court. It contains the same complex technology now used in modern Federal District courts. Sophisticated audio and video recording systems, document cameras, annotation monitors, and plasma screens allow students to perfect their electronic trial skills by reviewing their courtroom performances with faculty members as they occur.

The Hotung Building also provides fifteen new faculty offices on the sixth floor. The Law Center's various institutes and its renowned Continuing Legal Education Program are located on the fifth floor. Two of Georgetown's ten law journals, the *International Environmental Law Review* and the *International Law Journal,* and various student organizations are located on the first floor. In keeping with the international theme of the Hotung Building, the Associate and Assistant Deans, the professional staff, and the support staff for our Office of International and Graduate Programs occupy the Yoshiyuki Takada Suite on the sixth floor. Takada is the president of the SMC Corporation, a progressive manufacturing company located in Tokyo, Japan. In 1997, Takada helped establish a chair in Asian Legal Studies at the Law Center in honor of James Morita, L'40; H'95, whose work with the Japanese community in Hawaii is instrumental to its welfare. Offices for the staff of the Law Center's International Summer School Programs in Florence and London and a resource library are also located in the suite. Finally, a graduate student lounge and information center are adjacent to the Takada Suite.

The Timothy and Linda O'Neill Alumni Welcome Center was created on the second floor of the Hotung Building overlooking the Tower Green to acknowledge the importance of the Law Center's alumni to its mission and to the success of the Campus Completion Project. The Welcome Center includes a library and business center for alumni visitors. The Alumni, Development, and Public Relations staff, along with reception areas, exhibit spaces, work spaces, and conference rooms are located both on the first floor and in the Welcome Center. The O'Neills are 1977 graduates of Georgetown, he from the Law Center and she from the School of Nursing. Mr. O'Neill practiced law as an associate at Donovan, Leisure, and Irvine in New York before joining Goldman Sachs as an investment banker in 1988. Mrs. O'Neill volunteers full-time at the Columbia Presbyterian Hospital and is a trustee, along with her husband, of the Timothy J. and Linda D. O'Neill Foundation. Placing the Alumni Center on the campus brings together for the first time all segments of the Law Center community and offers students unparalleled access to the alumni. We hope that the Alumni Center will connect the students of today with the students of the past in ways that will encourage an understanding of the Law Center's history and permit alumni to guide students who are contemplating their future life and work.

The celebration tomorrow ties together our past, our present, and our future. It marks the end of a half century of academic achievement and physical expansion, and summons dreams of greater challenges and achievement. Georgetown's initial investment in the East End thirty-five years ago was the catalyst for the vibrant neighborhood that grows around us today. Since our arrival in 1971, hotels, residences, restaurants, and retailers have joined the Law Center to completely transform our neighborhood. By leading this East End renaissance, Georgetown reaffirmed the commitment it made to Washington, D.C., in 1870, when it chose to locate its law school in the heart of the city rather than on Georgetown University's hilltop campus.

As we contemplate the reinvigorated campus today, we are reminded of that commitment and our history. The Tower Green that now encompasses the old F Street reminds us that our prior buildings were located on various streets in the original L'Enfant plan. Looking north from the Hotung Building, we see Gonzaga High School's first building in the East End, still standing on I Street, NW, but now surrounded by other Gonzaga buildings which provide a testament to their own history of growth. Looking at our academic neighbors, we are reminded that a century ago Gonzaga vacated the old Washington Seminary at 9th and F Streets, NW, and offered the building to the Law Center for its second home. Looking east, Union Station reminds us of Washington, D.C.'s post-Civil War rebirth and of the McMillan Commission's revitalization plan that married the Beaux Arts movement to the L'Enfant plan at the beginning of the twentieth century. To the west we see the Holy Rosary Church and hear the bells ringing from its campanile, reminding us of the immigrants, former slaves, and all of their children who occupied our East End neighborhood between the end of the Civil War and the beginning of the disastrous era of urban renewal. When we look south, we see the majestic U.S. Capitol Dome, reminding us that the city of Pierre L'Enfant and George Washington is a tribute to the great democratic experiment of the eighteenth-century philosophers and patriots, and a monument to the rule of law which we study every day. Each day into the future, the vistas we see from this Hotung International Law Building will remind us anew of our history in Washington and of our enduring commitment to this city and to the world.

The old East End, a neighborhood once teeming with life and then abandoned, is now restored. Together, we and our neighbors look to the future; we await stories yet to be told and dreams yet to be fulfilled. Dreams of academic excellence and civic virtue dance in the minds of our Georgetown Law Center community, while dreams of hope and prosperity linger in the air of the old East End. Our past and our pursuit of global understanding and justice link us to this neighborhood and to the rest of the world. It is our duty to remember those who once lived here and to hold the land and Georgetown's aspirations in trust for those who will follow us.

As the Campus Completion Project comes to its end, so do these stories. To those of you who have wandered with me through Georgetown's history and architectural achievements, I hope you have enjoyed reading these stories as much as I have enjoyed sharing them with you.

END NOTES

Some websites have been taken down between the time this book was researched and the time it was published. Some of them can be retrieved by using the Internet Archive at http://www.archive.org/web/web.php.

1. "Campus Completion Project – Construction Notes": http://www.law.georgetown.edu/ccp/notes.html (visited June 29, 2005).

2. Carroll was well-known by the founding fathers and mothers of the country. At that time, the Pope had disbanded the Jesuits, so Georgetown was not officially a Jesuit school. Once the order was restored, the principles of Jesuit education imbued the school.

3. "Georgetown University History": http://guide.georgetown.edu/slideshows/slides/show11_slide5.html (visited June 29, 2005).

4. The Law Center was founded by a group of Maryland lawyers who believed that Georgetown needed a law department to provide students with a full complement of studies. Daniel R. Ernst, *The First 125 Years: An Illustrated History of The Georgetown University Law Center* (Washington, D.C.: Georgetown University Law Center, 1995), 7.

5. "Introduction to Pile-driving and Driven Piles": http://www.piledrivinghelp.com/pdpb-1.pdf (visited June 1, 2005). See generally, Don C. Warrington, *Pile-driving by Pile Buck* (ed. 2004).

6. Dr. K. Rainer Massarsch, "Deep Compaction of Granular Soils," International Lecture Series on Geotechnical Engineering and Its Development in the 21st Century, Zhejiang University, January 21, 1999, ch. 2, sec. 1, available at: http://www.geoforum.com/knowledge/texts/compaction/viewpage.asp?ID=8 (visited June 18, 2005).

7. Lindsay Falck, "Architecture 532 – Review Notes on Site Investigations," 4-5, available at: http://dolphin.upenn.edu/~falckda/assignments/532%20site%20Invest.doc (visited June 3, 2005).

8. Marshall Brain, "How Tower Cranes Work," available at: http://science.howstuffworks.com/tower-crane.htm (visited June 3, 2005).

9. Ibid.

10. The Piedmont Plateau was formed by the folding of rock layers caused by the collision of the North American and African tectonic plates. The heat and pressure caused by the movement of the Earth's crust transforms igneous and sedimentary rocks into metamorphic rocks. In the District's portion of the Piedmont, examples of metamorphic rock include gneiss and schist. Susan Woodward, "Appalachian Highlands: 1. Piedmont Plateau," available at: http://www.radford.edu/~swoodwar/CLASSES/GEOG202/physprov/piedmont.html (visited July 8, 2005). "How Rocks Are Formed": http://www.rocksforkids.com/RFK/howrocks.html (visited July 8, 2005). Jonathan Edwards, Jr., "A Brief Description of the Geology of Maryland," prepared by the Maryland Geological Survey (Baltimore: State of Maryland Department of Natural Resources, 1981).

11. Scientists do not know the exact causes of ice ages, or long-term climate changes in general, but plate tectonics are thought to play a major role. Plate motions lead to changes in topography, ocean currents, and the amount of carbon dioxide in the atmosphere, all of which have an effect on global climate. The existence or absence of mountains affects precipitation and wind. Ocean currents distribute heat around the planet, so changes in circulation can affect the polar regions. Carbon dioxide in the air causes the greenhouse effect which increases the mean global temperature. "NOVA Online/Cracking the Ice Age/ The Big Chill": http://www.pbs.org/wgbh/nova/ice/chill.html (visited July 8, 2005).

12. Thomas Jefferson, coming to Washington to assume the presidency, almost fell into the Tiber Creek when a bridge collapsed during one of the creek's many recurring floods.

13. Swampoodle was once a shanty town and home to a large Irish immigrant community. St. Aloysius Church and Gonzaga High School are now the only remnants of the old neighborhood, but establishments such as the Dubliner and Irish Times, both near the intersection of North Capitol and F Streets, bring a flavor of the old community to the area. "Early Irish Neighborhoods": http://www.rootsweb.com/~dcgenweb/body_irish.html (visited July 8, 2005).

14. Animal life included freshwater mollusks, turtles, crocodiles, and dinosaurs. Plant fossils include ferns, sequoia, water-lily, and grape. Slightly later deposits include shark teeth and leaves of oak, sumac, elm, holly, and blueberry. M. Carr, "The District of Columbia, Its Rocks and Their Geologic History," *U.S. Geological Survey Bulletin* (Washington, D.C.: Government Printing Office, 1950). Conversation with Ellis Yochelson, formerly of the United States Geological Survey and now Research Associate at the Smithsonian Museum of Natural History.

15. The Piedmont was formed during the Paleozoic era. Susan Woodward, "Appalachian Highlands: 1. Piedmont Plateau," available at: http://www.radford.edu/~swoodwar/CLASSES/GEOG202/physprov/ piedmont.html (visited July 8, 2005).

16. Iris Miller, *Washington in Maps* (New York: Rizzoli International Publications, Inc., 2002), 24.

17. The first Jesuits in the area landed on St. Clement's Island in the lower Potomac on March 25, 1634. Led by Father Andrew White, they came to America to escape religious persecution, minister to the colonists, and convert Native Americans. Father White worked extensively with the Piscataway Indians, learning their language and customs. He ultimately created an entire catechism in their native language, and in 1639 he established a mission at their tribal capital. "The Maryland Province of the Society of Jesus: Maryland Province History": http://www.marprovjesuits.org/province/history.shtml (visited July 19, 2005). "Catholic Encyclopedia: Piscataway Indians": http://www.newadvent.org/cathen/12114a.htm (visited July 19, 2005).

18. Like the Tyrannosaurus rex, the Capitalsaurus was a big, carnivorous reptile. Its name literally means "Capital reptile." Little else is known about it since the 1898 discovery of its vertebra is the only one on record. Those fossils were discovered during an excavation to lay a sewer pipe. Outside of D.C., dinosaur remains have often been found in clay deposits along U.S. Route 1 in Prince George's and Anne Arundel counties in an area known as "Dinosaur Alley." "Is Capitalsaurus the real thing?," *Washington Post*, Curriculum Guide: Dinosaurs, June 10, 2003, vol. 2, issue 5, available at: http://www.washpost.com/ nielessonplans.nsf/bydate (visited July 11, 2005).

19. Meridian Hill Park, now called Malcolm X Park, exhibits neoclassical influences in its long greens, cascading waters, and various statues dotting the landscape. During L'Enfant's planning stages, Thomas Jefferson proposed siting the Executive Mansion, now the White House, on the prime meridian of the United States (the Greenwich Meridian was not adopted as the sole world meridian until 1884). Located roughly on 16th Street, NW, the Washington meridian runs north from the White House to the park and lends its name to both the hill and the park. "Meridian Hill/ Malcolm X Park History": http://www. washingtonparks.net/meridianhillhistory.html (visited July 8, 2005).

20. Burnham rose to fame after 1892 when he managed the construction of the Columbian Exposition in Chicago. The buildings reintroduced classic forms into American architecture, creating the City Beautiful movement. The City Beautiful Movement sought to eliminate social ills by improving living conditions in American cities through architecture based on European styles.

21. It also eliminated a train station at the corner of New Jersey Avenue and C Street, NW.

22. Although the city's layout is commonly known as "L'Enfant's plan," L'Enfant was dismissed by President Washington after only one year for troubles caused by his temperamental nature and stubbornness. He had a grand vision for the new city, but it was subject to frequent revisions which did not play well with the politics of establishing and funding a new federal city. Believing that he only had to answer to President Washington, L'Enfant also had difficulty working with surveyor Andrew Ellicott of Baltimore and the commissioners entrusted by Congress with building the national city. Thus, although originally handpicked by President Washington to lay out the city, L'Enfant was ultimately, but regretfully, dismissed by the same man for the sake of expediency and to head off attempts to keep the capital in Philadelphia. Constance McLaughlin Green, *Washington: A History of the Capital, 1800-1950*, vol. 1 (Princeton: Princeton University Press, 1962), 14.

23. The Washington, D.C. Downtown Action Agenda was established to revitalize the city's downtown area by improving public transportation and increasing housing and economic development. See "Downtown Action Agenda Report": http://planning.dc.gov/planning/frames.asp?doc=/planning/LIB/planning/project/ downtown_ap/do cs/ch1.pdf (visited June 29, 2005).

24. The National Association of Realtors building, new convention center, Regal Cinema at Gallery Place, and the Meridian at Gallery Place and Mass Court apartment buildings which house many law students have all been built since the Downtown Action Agenda was first unveiled by Mayor Anthony Williams in 2000. Two new museums have opened: the Spy Museum at F and 9th Streets, NW, and the City Museum at the historic Carnegie Library at Mount Vernon Square. The proposed Downtown Circulator bus system started

in July 2005 with an east-west route running from Union Station to Georgetown and a north-south component running from the new convention center at Mount Vernon Square down 7th Street, NW, through the Mall to the Southwest Waterfront. The following projects are still under construction: the Newseum building at Pennsylvania and 6th Street, NW, scheduled to open in 2006; development of the Mather Building at 9th and G Streets, NW; development of the old National Wax Museum site at 5th and K Streets, NW; and development of the old convention center site on New York between 9th and 11th Streets. "DC Circulator": http://dccirculator.com/interactive_map.htm (visited July 20, 2005). "The Newseum's Move to Washington, D.C.": http://www.newseum.org/newseum/newseum2006/index.htm (visited July 20, 2005). "D.C. Department of Housing and Community Development - News Room": http://www.dhcd.dcgov.org/news/2001/08/08_28_01.shtm (visited July 20, 2005). "Neighborhood Development Company/NDC In the News!": http://www.neighborhooddevelopment.com/news_story14.html (visited July 20, 2005).

25. "Concrete," Encyclopedia Britannica Premium Service, available at: http://www.britannica.com/eb/article?tocId=9025103 (visited June 30, 2005). "building construction," Encyclopedia Britannica Premium Service, available at: http://www.britannica.com/eb/article?tocId=59310 (visited June 30, 2005).

26. At the dawn of the nineteenth century, Washington had to constantly defend itself against proposals to move the capital to the more established city of Philadelphia, assumptions that it would never become a commercially viable location, and unrest amongst local citizens about their lack of political representation in the new government. After Washington's humiliating defeat and torching of its public buildings during the War of 1812, relocation of the capital to Philadelphia was again a hot topic. Only patriotism and a half-million-dollar loan from Washington bankers saved Washington's status as the nation's capital. Following the Civil War, Washington's decline in business, lack of urban conveniences, and resistance to racial equality prompted proposals to move the capital to the Midwest, where the new heart of America lay. Missouri Senator Logan proposed moving the Capital to St. Louis. Green, pages 30, 64-65, 293, 328.

27. See generally, Constance McLaughlin Green, *Washington: A History of the Capital, 1800-1950* (Princeton: Princeton University Press, 1962).

28. Ibid., vol. 1, 345. When the Territory of the District of Columbia was granted its own government in 1871, Alexander Shepherd was appointed by President Grant to the board of public works. An visionary with a larger-than-life personality, Shepherd quickly became the "Boss" of the board of public works and set about on a grand plan to modernize the District. From the beginning, citizens were alarmed by the cost of the plan and how quickly it was moving forward; however, Shepherd was adept at assuring his critics. Armed with his assurances and secretly expecting Congress to foot at least half of the cost, Shepherd plunged the city into debt and numerous construction projects. He insisted that work begin all over the city simultaneously to prevent piecemeal execution and the adoption of pay-as-you-go funding. Because he lacked engineering expertise and refused to wait for proper assessment of technical problems, many blunders resulted such as newly paved roads being dug up to lay a forgotten sewer line. Despite the downfalls of Shepherd's modus operandi, the improvements were visible enough by the spring of 1873 to impress visitors and encourage both public and private real estate development. However, when the bills finally came due in July 1873, the District found itself bankrupt and Congress quickly voted to end the territorial government. Ibid., vol. 1, 340-62.

29. Ibid., vol. 1, 346-52, 362.

30. Ibid., vol. 2, 83. Shepherd's statue was reinstalled in January 2005 in front of the District of Columbia's John A. Wilson Building after being in storage since 1979.

31. Daniel R. Ernst, *The First 125 Years: An Illustrated History of The Georgetown University Law Center* (Washington, D.C.: Georgetown University Law Center, 1995), 10-11.

32. Ibid., 15.

33. Ibid.

34. Each time Georgetown considered a new home, the issue arose again. Sometimes Georgetown administrators were not interested in having us move to the main campus. Alumni generally favored the downtown campus, even though some faculty would have preferred moving closer to the faculty of other disciplines.

35. Carriage roads were built and remain under the East entrance to the Capitol. According to L'Enfant's original plan, he intended East Capitol Street to be a wide boulevard (160 feet in width) with arches on either side for merchants to set up shop. He also indicated that a column was to be placed at the street's terminus one mile east of the Capitol where Lincoln Park is now located. The column was to serve as a marker from which all distances in the United States were to be calculated. This "Zero Milestone" marker

ended up being placed on the South Lawn of the White House in 1919 in a send-off ceremony for the U.S. Army's first cross-continent convoy to the West Coast. As part of the 1919 convoy, future president Dwight D. Eisenhower observed firsthand the importance of good roads and the need for an interstate highway system. When he became president, he started building America's highway system and considered it one of his most important accomplishments in office. Iris Miller, pages 38-39. "Zero Milestone - Washington, DC": http://www.fhwa.dot. gov/infrastructure/zero.htm (visited July 23, 2005).

36. In his landmark book on Washington's lost buildings, James M. Goode cites I. Cranford Neilson as the architect. [James M. Goode, *Capital Losses: A Cultural History of Washington's Destroyed Buildings* (Washington, D.C.: Smithsonian Institution Press, 1979), 224-25. This information is unchanged in his second edition, (Washington and London: Smithsonian Books, 2003) 257.] However, I believe the correct name is J. Crawford Neilson and that Goode's reference possibly stems from the difficulty of interpreting an old document, possibly handwritten. Goode's files at the Washington Historical Society shed no light on the discrepancy in spelling. No other references to an architect by the name of I. Cranford Neilson seem to exist, while J. Crawford Neilson was indeed a Baltimore architect who designed railroad stations for the Baltimore & Ohio Railroad, as well as commercial buildings, several churches, and both country homes and townhouses for the well-to-do, many of whom were in fact directors of the B&O Railroad. He was also a founding member of the Baltimore Chapter of the American Institute of Architects (AIA) at its charter in 1870. "The Baltimore Architecture Foundation": http://www.baltimorearchitecture.org/bios/neilson_jc.html (visited September 16, 2005). I have consulted members of the foundation who were writing a book about J. Crawford Neilson and they have consulted Washington architectural historian and writer Pamela Scott. Based on the style and the time period, they believe that J. Crawford Neilson was likely the designer of the American Colonization Society building, although the Baltimore Architectural Foundation has yet to state definitively that their man was the architect of the Colonization Society hall. E-mail from James T. Wollon, Jr., AIA, Vice President for Research, on file with author.

37. Richardson's interpretation of the Romanesque style made it distinctly American. He kept the rounded arches surrounding doors and windows, but his buildings had a heavier look to them because they were more horizontal in nature and had textured masonry facades. The massiveness of this style was perfect for buildings designed to impress upon a visitor the nature of the American character. Thus, Richardson Romanesque became popular for churches and university buildings as well as public buildings such as railroad stations and courthouses. John C. Poppeliers, S. Allen Chambers, Jr., and Nancy B. Schwartz, *What Style Is It?: A Guide to American Architecture* (Washington, D.C.: Preservation Press, 1983), 62-65.

38. Bushrod Washington founded the American Colonization Society along with Presbyterian minister Robert Finley, Francis Scott Key, and Henry Clay, and served as the society's first president. He was also the nephew of George Washington and an associate justice of the Supreme Court from 1798 to 1829. Upon the deaths of George and Martha Washington, Bushrod inherited Mount Vernon and assisted John Marshall on his biography of George Washington. "Washington, Bushrod," Encyclopedia Britannica Online School Edition, available at: http://school.eb.com/eb/article?tocId=9076187 (visited July 24, 2005). "American Colonization Society," Encyclopedia Britannica Online School Edition, available at: http://school.eb.com/eb/article?tocId=9006105 (visited July 24, 2005).

39. The West African colony of Maryland was established by the Maryland branch of the American Colonization Society. Maryland was joined with its neighbor Liberia in 1857 to form the nation of Liberia, which is now the oldest democracy in Africa. Goode, (1979), pages 224-25.

40. John Russell Pope revived many different architectural styles, but in Washington, D.C., he is most known for his Neoclassical designs, as demonstrated by the National Archives, Constitution Hall, the Jefferson Memorial, and the Scottish Rite Temple. Pope studied at the American Academy in Rome and the Ecole des Beaux-Arts. "Pope, John R.," Encyclopedia Britannica Online School Edition, available at: http://school.eb.com/eb/article?tocId=9060839 (visited July 24, 2005). Christopher Weeks, *AIA Guide to the Architecture of Washington, D.C.*, third ed. (Baltimore: Johns Hopkins University Press, 1994), 61-62, 68-69, 86, 152, 267-68.

41. Practicing the International Style of architecture, Chinese-born American architect I.M. Pei made his mark on Washington, D.C. in the 1970s with his characteristic use of simple geometric forms in complex arrangements. While the East Wing of the National Gallery of Art is one of his most famous works, Pei is also known around town for the Christian Science Church and the commercial buildings at L'Enfant Plaza. "Pei, I.M.," Encyclopedia Britannica Online School Edition, available at: http://school.eb.com/eb/article?tocId=9058960 (visited July 24, 2005). Weeks, pages 16, 69.

42. Over Presidents' Day weekend in 2003, Washington, D.C. and the rest of the Northeast was blanketed with over two feet of snow in a massive snowstorm. The airports, monuments, memorials, the entire

Smithsonian Institution, and most shopping malls closed their doors. The District, Virginia, and Maryland all declared a state of emergency while the snow threatened to break records set in 1922. Snow removal crews were overwhelmed throughout the region for several days. "Area Closed on Account of Snow; Blizzard of '03 Overwhelms Roads, Rails," *Washington Post*, February 17, 2003.

43. "Wilson Bridge Work a Balancing Act," *Washington Post*, December 8, 2002.

44. Goode, (1979), page 194.

45. In 1792, James Hoban won the design competition and commission for the President's House, which he based on the Palladian styles seen in English and Irish houses such as the Leinster House in Dublin. After the British torched it in 1814, the building was restored by Hoban and painted white for the first time to disguise its charred surface; however, it was not officially named the White House until 1901 when President Theodore Roosevelt began using the term. Hoban also built both the semicircular South Portico and the more formal North Portico. Weeks, pages 130-31.

46. Morris J. MacGregor, *A Parish for the Federal City: St. Patrick's in Washington, 1794-1994* (Washington, D.C.: Catholic University of America Press, 1994), 68, n. 22.

47. Ibid., 76, 78-79, 127, 177, n. 47.

48. Lawrence O'Connor also built other Catholic buildings in his home state of New York. For the Sisters of the Divine Compassion in White Plains, NY, he worked with Mother Mary Veronica to construct the Chapel of Divine Compassion, Good Counsel Convent, and House of Nazareth in Italianate and Spanish Mission revival styles. The entire Good Counsel Complex was placed on the National and State Registers of Historic Places in 1997. Unfortunately, he is mistakenly credited under the name "O'Conner." "Sisters of the Divine Compassion: Tour of Historic Buildings": http://divinecompassion.org/tour.htm#index (visited July 25, 2005). "National Register of Historic Places: New York, Westchester County," available at: http://www.nationalregisterofhistoricplaces.com/NY/Westchester/state2.html (visited July 25, 2005).

49. Owen A. Hill and Gonzaga College, *Gonzaga College, An Historical Sketch; From Its Foundation in 1821 to the Solemn Celebration of Its First Centenary in 1921* (Washington, D.C.: The College, 1922), 22.

50. Ibid., 24-25, 33-34.

51. Very little is known about why the Washington Seminary, as a school for young boys, received the ability to confer degrees under its new name, Gonzaga College. There were no objections to the proposed bill nor any debate recorded in either the House Journal, Senate Journal, or Congressional Globe of the 35th Congress. Only one amendment was made, changing the value of real estate the school was able to hold from $500,000 to $200,000. As the school's enrollment grew, one may surmise that the school sought its own charter to gain freedom from Georgetown College's control. S. 76, 35th Cong. (1858). *Congressional Globe*, 35th Cong., 1st sess. 1867 (April 29, 1858).

52. Although Joseph Wildrich von Kammerhueber is not as well known as Adolf Cluss, the two men worked together on many civil projects, such as the Franklin and Sumner Schools, the first Department of Agriculture building, and Calvary Baptist Church at 8th and H Streets, NW. In 1864, the two men also recommended transforming the Washington Canal into a sewer system which sparked the creation of the Board of Public Works and "Boss" Shepherd's reign. "Adolf Cluss Biography": http://www.goethe.de/ins/us/was/pro/vtour/dc1/clussbio.htm (visited July 28, 2005). "Calvary Baptist Church": http://www.goethe.de/ins/us/was/pro/vtour/dc1/B1/09/en_index.htm (visited July 28, 2005). "Engineer in Washington, DC": http://www.adolf-cluss.org/index.php?lang=en&content=w&topSub=adolf&sub=1.4 (visited July 28, 2005).

53. Adolf Cluss made it big when he was appointed chief engineer for the Board of Public Works under "Boss" Shepherd. In addition to his collaborations with von Kammerhueber, Cluss also designed Eastern Market and the Smithsonian Arts and Industries Building among his many other distinctive red brick creations. His buildings had the latest technological advances and incorporated function into form. Although Cluss designed seventy-five buildings in D.C., only eight remain standing. In 2005, we are commemorating the 100th anniversary of his death in both Washington, D.C. and in his birthplace, Heilbronn, Germany. A series of lectures in Washington, and an exhibition called "Adolf Cluss: from Germany to America, Shaping a Capital City Worthy of a Republic" focuses on his life and work. Among the many interesting tidbits unbeknownst to many Washingtonians is that Cluss was a friend of Karl Marx and a communist revolutionary in his homeland of Germany and in the United States. In time, however, his pragmatism overcame his revolutionary proclivities and he became a staunch republican. Nonetheless, his belief in a classless society may have been the reason that he designed award-winning schools for both white and African American children. Cluss lived on Second Street, NW, between D and E Streets, just south of the Law Center's current home. "Celebrating Cluss: The Radical Red Father of Eastern Market," *Voice of the*

Hill, vol. 7, no. 4, July 2005. "An Architect for the Nation's Capital": http://www.adolf-cluss.org/ index.php?lang=en&content=w&topSub=adolf&sub=1.5 (visited July 28, 2005). "Wallach and Franklin Schools," *Cluss Newsletter*, December 2003, available at: http://www.goethe.de/ins/us/was/pro/vtour/ clussnewsletter/aclusstwo.htm (visited July 28, 2005).

54. They moved to new quarters at New York Avenue and 15th Street, NW, a building that now houses the National Museum of Women in the Arts.

55. Recent excavations for a new commercial development in the area appear to have discovered the Seminary's original foundations.

56. The story of the Gallaudets' ownership comes from personnel at successors to the Equitable Bank. I have not been able to verify their ownership otherwise.

57. Frederick Pyle designed Cleveland Park's last country house in 1914, called The Homestead (La Quinta). Located at 2700 Macomb Street, it was purchased in 1945 under India's new sovereignty to house India's ambassador. Arthur Heaton's work included a diverse range of projects: the National Dry Cleaning Institute in Silver Spring; the Park and Stop, a shopping center geared towards car owners in Cleveland Park; the Burleith residential development north of Georgetown; and Corcoran Hall, which was the first building on George Washington University's Foggy Bottom campus. In 1937, Heaton also served as the first chairman of the board of the new Washington Building Congress. "Montgomery Preservation Inc. Endangered Sites List": http://www.montgomerypreservation.org/Endangered02.html#DryCleaning (visited July 28. 2005). "Cleveland Park Historic District": http://www.cr.nps.gov/nr/travel/wash/dc4.htm (visited July 28, 2005). "Buildings: A Historical Overview – GW Historical Almanac – University Archives: Corcoran Hall": http://www.gwu.edu/gelman/archives/almanac/highlight.html#Corcoran (visited July 28, 2005). "October Bulletin: Six Decades of Service to Washington's Building Industry": http://www.wbcnet.org/OCT.HTM (visited July 28, 2005). "Burleith: History": http://www.burleith.org/history.html (visited July 28, 2005).

58. Shotcrete is concrete that is sprayed onto a surface by way of special equipment.

59. *Modern Steel Construction* (December 2000) (quoting *The Ironworker* (December 1984)).

60. Ibid. In the ten years from its beginning until the stock market crashed in 1929, the American Plan devastated union membership nationwide down to a level of nine percent of workers. Albert Lannon, "Building Our Unions: The 'American Plan' Hits Oakland," February 22, 1999, available at: http://www. hartford-hwp.com/archives/45b/072.html (visited July 28, 2005).

61. Feng shui literally means "wind and water" and is the ancient Chinese practice of living in harmony with one's environment such that the invisible energy or *ch'i* (pronounced 'chee') that surrounds the occupant is harnessed. The factors include the individual's birth year, compass orientations, and the placement of objects in the environment. Lillian Too, *Smart Feng Shui for the Home* (London: Element Books, 2001), 14, 15, 17, 157.

62. Ibid., 10. *Ch'i* (pronounced 'chee') is the invisible energy or "life breath" that surrounds an environment and is symbolically likened to a dragon's breath.

63. Abe Pollin is a developer and sports entrepreneur in Washington, D.C. He built the MCI Center (renamed the Verizon Center in March 2006) downtown and owns the Washington Wizards.

64. We experienced no fatalities and few injuries during the life of the Campus Completion Project.

65. "Steel," Encyclopedia Britannica Premium Service, available at: http://www.britannica.com/eb/ article?tocId=81449 (visited June 29, 2005).

66. Iris Miller, page 40.

67. Roger K. Lewis, "Testing the Upper Limits of D.C. Building Height Act," *Washington Post*, April 23, 1994.

68. Building Height Act of 1910, 36 Stat. 452 (codified as amended at D.C. Code Ann. 6-601.05 (2001).

69. Kirstin Downey, "Bethlehem Steel Corp. Is No More; Name Dies After Firm Is Sold Amid Industry Turmoil," *Washington Post*, May 1, 2003.

70. In early June 2005, D.C. experienced major thunderstorms that flooded streets and caused creeks to overflow. Lightning struck utility poles, and 60-mph gusts of wind blew roofs off and knocked down trees and power lines. Manny Fernandez and Jose Antonio Vargas, "Appraisals and Appreciations; Amid New Storms, Residents Assess Damage and Good Fortune," *Washington Post*, June 14, 2003. The weather during the life of this project was especially uncooperative. The snowy, cold winters and the many spring rains during construction caused the project to run out of the "weather delay days" usually factored into a contract

when determining the proposed completion date. As a result, the contract was amended to give Whiting-Turner another six weeks to complete the project without suffering penalties for delayed completion.

71. In 1985, National Savings and Trust Bank was acquired by Crestar Financial Corporation of Richmond which was subsequently acquired by SunTrust Banks, Inc. of Atlanta in 1998. Beth Berselli and Peter Behr, "Crestar to Be Acquired By Atlanta's SunTrust; Role in Area Won't Change, Va. Bank's Chief Says," *Washington Post*, July 21, 1998.

72. James S. Easby-Smith, *Georgetown University in the District of Columbia, 1789-1907: Its Founders, Benefactors, Officers, Instructors and Alumni*, vol. 1 (New York: The Lewis Pub. Co., 1907), 425, 433.

73. Ibid., 441.

74. "The Law Department," *Georgetown College Journal*, vol. xii, no. 2, November 1883, 17.

75. Easby-Smith, page 446.

76. There is some evidence, although not conclusive, that the home once belonged to the family of George Hamilton, an early Dean of the Law School.

77. "The New Law Building," *Georgetown College Journal*, vol. xii, no. 4, January 1884, 61.

78. The Second Empire style was named for the reign of Napoleon III, whose transformation of Paris into a grandiose city was emulated throughout Europe. His most famous building project, the enlargement of the Louvre, revived a roof design which was created by the seventeenth-century French Renaissance architect, Francois Mansart. The mansard roof is a roof that has two slopes on all four sides. The two slopes, that is, the double-pitched nature of the roof, creates more head room in the attic making it more usable. Other Second Empire features include, the balustrade (a rail supported by uprights which are often vase-shaped); the pavilion (part of a building projecting from the external wall); the dormer (a vertical window set into a sloping roof); the pediment (a triangular decorative piece placed over doors and windows); and paired columns supporting entablatures (decorative elements placed between columns and the roof). Poppeliers, Chambers, and Schwartz, pages 52-55.

79. Several conspirators were tried for their role in Lincoln's assassination. Mrs. Surratt, the first woman hanged in the United States, went to the gallows with several others. One, Dr. Samuel A. Mudd, who set Booth's leg when he arrived at Mudd's farm in Bryantown, Maryland, had attended Georgetown University for one year before going to the University of Maryland to study medicine. His trial following the assassination was one of the most controversial, with his supporters insisting that he was just a country doctor who treated a stranger in need. Despite the controversy, he was sentenced to life in federal prison at Dry Tortugas, Florida, avoiding the death penalty by a single vote. When yellow fever broke out in the prison in 1867 and claimed the prison doctor's life, Dr. Mudd became the new prison doctor until he was pardoned by President Andrew Johnson in 1869 because of his efforts during the epidemic. Upon his release, he came back to Maryland, and in 1876, he was elected to the state legislature. "Biography and Images of Dr. Samuel Mudd, Assassination Conspirator": http://www.law.umkc.edu/faculty/projects/ftrials/lincolnconspiracy/mudd.html (visited September 15, 2005).

80. Archeological evidence of Mary Ann Hall's brothel was discovered during excavations for the new National Museum of the American Indian. Artifacts such as expensive porcelain pieces, champagne corks, bones from choice cuts of meat, and women's grooming products, in addition to her 1840 census report, listed as the head of the household of six females and one male slave, point to the conclusion that Mary Ann ran an expensive brothel. "Madam on the Mall": http://www.si.edu/oahp/madam/ (visited July 29, 2005).

81. In addition to her many "firsts," Belva Ann Lockwood also drafted a successful bill that required equal pay for female federal employees, sponsored the first African American from the South for admission to the Supreme Court bar, and served on the Nobel Peace Prize nominating committee. Lockwood also argued on behalf of Cherokee Indians in *Cherokee Nation v. United States* and won about $5 million for her clients. Barbara Babcock, "Belva Ann Lockwood: For Peace, Justice, and President," available at: http://www.stanford.edu/group/WLHP/papers/lockwood.htm (visited July 29, 2005).

82. George Washington wanted to establish a national university in the new capital and left stock shares in his will for an endowment; but even into the 1820s, Washingtonians were still longing for a national university. Columbian College started the first law program in D.C. in 1826, but had to close it after one year due to lack of finances and low student enrollment. It reopened in 1865 and had sixty graduates in its first graduating class. It gained university status in 1873 and became Columbian University. In 1904, it was renamed George Washington University. Founded in 1869, National University Law School focused on legal education within D.C. It merged with George Washington University Law School in 1954. Belva A. Lockwood received her law degree from National University in 1872. By the end of the 1800s, however,

the school was no longer accepting female applicants. This state of affairs prompted two women attorneys to start the Washington College of Law, the first law school created for women and by women. It merged with American University in 1949. "The Law School: Chronology and Recent Deans – GW Historical Almanac – University Archives": http://www.gwu.edu/gelman/archives/almanac/deans/lawschl.html (visited July 29, 2005). "The George Washington University Law School: A Brief History": http://www.law.gwu.edu/About /A+Brief+History.htm (visited July 29, 2005). "Washington College of Law: Rich in History - Timeline": http://law.american.edu/history/timeline.cfm (visited July 29, 2005).

83. Easby-Smith, page 441.

84. Ibid. at 442.

85. For example, it is hard to think about Chicago without thinking about the Chicago school architects who built skyscrapers at the turn of the twentieth century. One cannot think about San Francisco without thinking about the Golden Gate Bridge. Our own Washington, D.C. is often defined by its neo-classical buildings and the Mall.

86. Faye Rice, "Do You Work In a Sick Building?," *Fortune*, July 2, 1990.

87. There are many myths about what caused the windows in Boston's Hancock Building to fall to the ground. The tower was swaying too much in the wind, its rhomboid shape was causing wind forces called "hot spots" to suck out the glass, or the settling foundation was stressing the windows. Even though all these speculated causes actually happened, they were not the real cause of the window problem. The problem lay in the windows' design. Each pane had a layer of air between two layers of glass, all surrounded by a metal frame. Tightly bonded to the metal frame was a coat of chromium placed inside to achieve the Hancock's distinctive mirror effect. Glass always moves due to temperature changes and wind vibrations, but because the frames were so tightly bonded, they were inflexible and unable to move without cracking. The cracks in the frames were then transmitted to the glass. Perhaps because of the high publicity, all the major players involved in this window disaster were required to sign a legal pact of silence. However, by talking with experts, Robert Campbell of the *Boston Globe* was able to piece together the mystery. Robert Campbell, "Builders Faced Bigger Crisis Than Falling Windows," *Boston Globe*, March 3, 1995.

88. In April 2001, a single steel roof truss was installed without temporary bracing, which requires stabilization of structural elements through welding or bolting. As a result, twelve steel roof trusses came crashing down due to nighttime gusts of wind. Fortunately, no one was injured. Manny Fernandez, "Improper Bracing Blamed in Collapse; 2 Reports Say D.C. Center Was Vulnerable to Wind," *Washington Post*, May 11, 2001.

89. BTU stands for British Thermal Unit. It is the standard used to measure heating capacity. It is the quantity of heat required to raise the temperature of one pound of water from 60 to 61F at a constant pressure of one atmosphere.

90. Easby-Smith, page 446.

91. Ibid., 422. The founders felt that a law department was a necessary addition to the existing program at Georgetown for the benefit of its graduates and the general public.

92. David Burnes bought the original land grant in 1721. It included over 500 acres of tobacco growing land that extended from the current H Street to Constitution Avenue, NW, and from 3rd Street to 18th Street. His own cottage, which stood until 1894, existed on the site now occupied by the Organization of American States. His daughter, Marcia, inherited all his property when he passed away and became the subject of many suitors as the richest woman in Washington, D.C. In 1802, she married John Peter Van Ness, the Representative from New York and future mayor of D.C., and dedicated her life and money to philanthropic work. She died while caring for sick children in the cholera epidemic of 1832 and was buried with her husband in a mausoleum modeled after the Temple of Vesta in Rome. Thomas Carrier, *Washington, D.C.: A Historical Walking Tour* (Charleston, S.C.: Arcadia Publishing, 1999), 92. "John Peter Van Ness": http:// www.famousamericans.net/johnpetervanness/ (visited September 15, 2005). "GORP: Biking in D.C. - Rock Creek Park": http://gorp.away.com/gorp/publishers/countryman/bik_new2.htm (visited September 15, 2005).

93. The old City Hall will soon become the home of the D.C. Court of Appeals, the city's highest local court. As the focal point of Judiciary Square, the old City Hall was the old D.C. Courthouse in a prior life. During that time, the building witnessed Daniel Webster and Francis Scott Key practicing law and the civil trial of John Surratt who was accused of taking part in the assassination of President Abraham Lincoln. John Surratt's mother, Mary Surratt, was tried by military tribunal and hanged just two years earlier at the Arsenal Penitentiary, located in Fort McNair. John had escaped to Canada and then to Europe, only to be apprehended in Alexandria, Egypt and brought back to trial in 1867. In the interim, the U.S. Supreme Court ruled that military courts had no jurisdiction over civilians when the civil courts were open. Ex parte Milligan, 71 U.S. 2 (1866). Because of the decision, John was able to have a civil trial instead of a military commission like his mother. With the resulting hung jury, he was perhaps saved from her fate as well. Annice Wagner, U.S. Senate Committee on Appropriations, D.C. Subcommittee Hearing, April 30, 2003, available at: http://appropriations.senate.gov/text/subcommittees/record.cfm?id=203407 (visited September 5, 2005). "Mary and John Surratt - A Narrative": http://www.surratt.org/su_hist.html (visited September 5, 2005). "Biography and Images of John Surratt, Assassination Conspirator": http://www.law.umkc.edu/faculty/projects/ftrials/lincolnconspiracy/surrattj.html (visited September 5, 2005)

94. As an honors graduate in engineering from West Point, Montgomery Meigs first came to Washington to work in the U.S. Army Corps of Engineers. His career included many engineering feats such as the Washington Aqueduct, which brought in water from Great Falls, Maryland and the Rock Creek Bridge in Georgetown. With his only son killed in combat during the Civil War, Meigs also recommended the Arlington grounds to be used as a cemetery for fallen Union soldiers. Goode, (1979) pages 72-76.

95. There are many stories about the old Pension Building. One involves the ghost of a dead cavalryman riding his horse down the stairs. Some believe that it is the ghost of Montgomery Meigs, watching over his architectural masterpiece, especially during periods of renovation. Pension Commissioner James Tanner, who lost both legs in the Second Battle of Bull Run, is rumored to limp along the building's upper levels. Buffalo Bill, aka William F. Cody, attended two presidential inaugural balls in the building and is rumored to have stated his desire to haunt the place. John Alexander, *Ghosts: Washington's Most Famous Ghost Stories* (Washington, D.C.: Washingtonian Books, 1987). "National Building Museum": http://www.mmdtkw.org/VNatBuildMus.html (visited July 31, 2005).

96. "The American Presidency: Life and Death in the White House": http://americanhistory.si.edu/presidency/3_frame.html (visited July 31, 2005).

97. Goode, (1979), pages 146-47, 168-70.

98. I could find little information about Denson. He designed several commercial and residential buildings in the Northwest section of Washington, D.C. beginning in 1885. One that still remains is the Atlantic Building at 930 F Street, NW, although it is currently being incorporated into a new development.

99. James R. Theirry, *A Partial History of The Georgetown University Law Center*, ch. 2 (unpublished), 19.

100. Picturesque eclecticism is a catch-all category for nineteenth-century domestic architecture that incorporated elements from many different styles, thus, an "eclectic" mix. Most of the borrowed elements came from the Second Empire and Queen Anne styles. Poppeliers, Chambers, and Schwartz, pages 52-53, 57.

101. "The School of Law," *Georgetown College Journal*, vol. xx, no. 3, December 1891, 61.

102. "The New Building of the School of Law," *Georgetown College Journal*, vol. xix, no. 8, May 1891, 143.

103. Ibid., 144.

104. *Georgetown University School of Law Bulletin* (1891-1892).

105. *Cushing v. Rodman*, 82 F.2d 864 (D.C. Cir. 1936). Rodman's restaurant lay at the corner of 5th and E Streets, NW, and was acquired by the Law Center and turned into a student lounge. Allan B. Luks, "The Law Center Story: Notes on The Evolution of A Legal Institution," *Georgetown Law Res Ipsa Loquitur*, 1964, 7.

106. The name change reflected the Law Center's expanding mission. During those years, administrators created several institutes and non-teaching programs to complement its teaching mission.

107. Coleman Nevils, *Miniatures of Georgetown, 1634-1934* (Washington, D.C.: Georgetown University Press, 1934), 226.

108. Easby-Smith, page 486.

109. Hamilton served as Dean for over 30 years, longer than any other Dean. Hugh Fegan served as Associate Dean for over 20 years, longer than any other Associate Dean. Paul Dean is considered the founding dean of the modern law school. He was appointed in 1954 and served 15 years. He became the school's leader as the power of the Jesuit Regent, Reverend Francis Edmund Lucey, dwindled. Lucey ran the school and taught for thirty-one years. Jaeger, Gordon, and Dugan were colorful teachers whose students still talk about them.

110. Paul Dean, *The Report of the Dean*, Georgetown University Law Center, 1962. Other quotes in this paragraph come from the same report.

111. I worked in the library while I was a law student. Books were everywhere. No one wanted to retrieve the books from the basement for fear they would have to fight with a rat to get them.

112. As the uprising began, smoke from the downtown area and from H Street, N.E. was visible from the top floors of the Law Center. The Law Center, like everything else downtown, was closed for several days. Once order was restored, the Law Center and its E. Barrett Prettyman fellows provided training for lawyers seeking to assist the hundreds of people who had been arrested.

113. In 1970, as Americans learned of President Nixon's broadening the war into Cambodia, students forced the closure of the school. Georgetown faculty and students, like those from other schools across the nation, agreed that they could not continue business as usual.

114. James Cross Giblin, *Let There Be Light: A Book About Windows* (New York: Thomas Y. Crowell, 1988) (quoting Jeremiah 9:21), 17.

115. Ibid.

116. Ibid.

117. "Window," Encyclopedia Britannica Online School Edition, available at: http://school.eb.com/eb/article-9077176 (visited July 31, 2005). The Hagia Sophia was built by Justinian after an earthquake destroyed Constantine's church. A marvel of architecture, the Hagia Sophia has suffered many more earthquakes since then, most recently in 1999, but still it stands.

118. Ibid.

119. Ibid.

120. Cames are the slender grooved lead bars that hold the panes in stained glass.

121. James Cross Giblin, pages 72-73.

122. A soffit is the underside of a structural component, such as a beam, arch, or cornice.

123. A stone on the U.S. Capitol grounds marks the location of the house.

124. Green, Vol. 1, page 337.

125. Henry James, *The American Scene* (London, 1907), 303

126. Douglas E. Evelyn and Paul Dickson, *On This Spot: Pinpointing the Past in Washington, D.C.* (Washington, D.C.: Farragut Publishing Co., 1992), 19.

127. "Law Commencement of Georgetown University," *Georgetown College Journal*, vol. ii, no. 8, July 1873, 88.

128. Evelyn and Dickson, pages 4-5.

129. Ibid.

130. "Washington Baseball Club: Photo History: Swampoodle Grounds": http://www.baseballindc.com/history/photos_sg.asp (visited July 31, 2005). President Benjamin Harrison was the first president to attend a major league baseball game, cheering on the Washington Nationals at Swampoodle Stadium. F. Ceresi, M. Rucker, & C. McMains, Images in America, Baseball in Washington, D.C.

131. My analysis is based on the location of the railroad track bed at the time. The other interpretation seems to be based on the current location of the tracks.

132. Green, vol. 1, pages 320-21.

133. Green, vol. 2, pages 340-41.

134. Ibid.

135. Elizabeth Brennan, "Preservation Online: D.C. School to be Reused": http://www.nationaltrust.org/magazine/archives/arc_news/021902.htm (visited July 31, 2005).

136. St. Patrick's was worried that the new parishes would decrease its congregation. Thus, the parishes built in the early 1900s were supposed to serve only their ethnic groups.

137. Mary Elizabeth Brown, *An Italian American Community of Faith, Holy Rosary in Washington, D.C.* (New York: Center for Migration Studies, 2004), 19-20.

138. Ibid.

139. The Jewish community has a renewed presence in downtown D.C. When the former home of the Adas Israel Congregation was put up for sale for possible commercial purposes, Abe Pollin and two other developers, Shelton Zuckerman and Douglas Jemal, were aghast and purchased the property. In 2004, the Sixth and I Historic Synagogue was rededicated after a $2.5 million renovation that also recreated many architectural details. Debbi Wilgoren, "Reviving Roots of a Community; All Jewish Branches To Use Synagogue," *Washington Post*, April 22, 2004.

140. Green, vol. 2, pages 396-98.

141. Camden Yards is the home of the Baltimore Orioles. It is approximately 30 miles from Washington, D.C.

142. Tom Inglesby, "Up We Go – Mast Climbing Work Platforms Reach for the Sky," *Masonry Magazine*, June 2002, available at: http://www.masonrymagazine.com/6-02/mastclimbers.html (visited July 31, 2005).

143. Ibid.

144. "The London Bridge Museum & Educational Trust: Glaziers Hall Limited": http://www.oldlondonbridge.com/glzh.shtml (visited July 31, 2005).

145. "Glassmaking at Jamestown": http://www.nps.gov/colo/Jthanout/Glassmak.html (visited July 31, 2005).

146. Ibid.

147. Ibid.

148. "New Jersey Scuba Diver - Artifacts & Shipwrecks - Glass": http://www.njscuba.net/artifacts/matl_glass.html (visited July 31, 2005).

149. "Industrial glass," Encyclopedia Britannica Online School Edition, available at: http://school.eb.com/eb/article-76378 (visited July 31, 2005). All quotes in this section are from this Britannica entry.

150. Giblin, page 31. Glassmaking production facilities dating from 1600 B.C. to 1500 B.C. have recently been found in Egypt. Guy Gugliotta, "Evidence of Glassmaking In Ancient Egypt Found," *Washington Post*, June 17, 2005.

151. Debbi Wilgoren, "A New Beginning for the District's East End; Residents Flock to Once-Empty Downtown Streets," *Washington Post*, March 7, 2004.

152. S. L. Fishbein, "No. 2 Leads City in Vice and Violence," *Washington Post - Times Herald*, March 14, 1954. This six-part series spawned many other articles during the next several years that led to calls for urban renewal. The quotes in the text are taken from several of those articles.

153. J. Eisen, "Northwest's Areas Seek Places in the Sun," *Washington Post*, January 1, 1958.

154. J. Scott, "2nd Precinct Gives Police Most Trouble," *Washington Post - Times Herald*, February 14, 1954.

155. J. Hoagland, "Ghost Town In Northwest Created By Renewal," *Washington Post*, November 24, 1967.

156. J. Scott, "2nd Precinct Gives Police Most Trouble," *Washington Post - Times Herald*, February 14, 1954.

157. S. L. Fishbein, "No. 2 Leads City in Vice and Violence," *Washington Post - Times Herald*, March 14, 1954.

158. J. White, "Some Eyesores Are Gone, Others Transferred," *Washington Post*, August 7, 1956.

159. Mary Elizabeth Brown, *An Italian American Community of Faith, Holy Rosary in Washington, D.C.* (New York: Center for Migration Studies, 2004), 114-16. As a graduate of Harvard Law School, Charles Hamilton Houston started taking on civil rights cases in Washington, D.C. In 1929, he was tapped to become the head of the Howard University School of Law, and he embarked on a path to train civil rights lawyers, the most famous being Thurgood Marshall. "Separate Is Not Equal: Charles Hamilton Houston": http://americanhistory.si.edu/brown/history/3-organized/charles-houston.html (visited July 31, 2005).

160. Shelley v. Kraemer, 334 U.S. 1 (1948).

161. During the post World War II era, Democrats often controlled the House and Senate and the leadership of the Democratic party was controlled by long-seated Southerners. The notorious Senator Theodore Bilbo of Mississippi often sat on the Senate District Committee. Congressman John McMillan of South Carolina chaired the House Committee for many years. *Congressional Directory* (Washington, D.C.: U.S. Government Printing Office). Garrison Nelson, *Committees in the U.S. Congress 1947-1992, Committee Jurisdictions and Member Rosters* (Washington, D.C.: Congressional Quarterly, 1993).

162. Linda Wheeler, "Broken Ground, Broken Hearts; In '50s, Many Lost SW Homes to Urban Renewal," *Washington Post*, June 21, 1999. The urban renewal plan was so devastating in displacing residents and destroying the neighborhood's character that it spawned a 1990 documentary called "Southwest Remembered" by producer/director Delores Smith and Lamont Productions.

163. Raze or repair orders were orders issued by the D.C. Housing authority to either repair the house to make it habitable or tear it down.

164. Serge F. Kovaleski and David A. Fahrenthold, "NW Housing Complex A Tangle of Drugs, Despair," *Washington Post*, February 1, 2004.

165. Ibid.

166. Ibid.

167. Lori Montgomery, "Sursum Corda Takes Offer From Developer," *Washington Post*, November 2, 2005.

168. Paul Dean, *The Report of the Dean*, Georgetown University Law Center, 1962.

169. Paul Dean, *The Report of the Dean*, Georgetown University Law Center, 1965-1966.

170. Ibid.

171. Ernst, page 87.

172. Ibid.

173. Ibid.

174. Eugene C. Murdock, *Bernard P. McDonough: The Man & His Work* (Marietta, Ohio: Marietta College Press, 1988), 10.

175. Ibid.

176. Ibid., 162.

177. Ibid., 163.

178. Ibid.

179. Ibid., 177.

180. "More Than Modern," *Time Magazine*, March 31, 1858.

181. The International Style of architecture began in the 1920s and 1930s and focused on functionality, discarding frivolous adornments. The style made good use of advances in structural and material sciences and predominantly used concrete, glass, and steel. International Style buildings tend to have clean lines and angles, overall balance, and a horizontal feel to them. Poppeliers, Chambers, and Schwartz, pages 92-95.

182. Edward Durell Stone, *The Evolution of An Architect* (New York: Horizon Press, 1962), 158.

183. "Edward Durell Stone," *Encyclopedia of World Biography*, 2nd ed. (Detroit: Gale, 1998).

184. Edward Durell Stone, *Recent and Future Architecture* (New York: Horizon Press, 1967), 10.

185. "Edward Durell Stone," *Encyclopedia of World Biography*, 2nd ed. (Detroit: Gale, 1998).

186. Paul Goldberger, "Edward Durell Stone Dead at 76; Designed Major Works Worldwide," *New York Times*, August 7, 1978.

187. Ibid.

188. Ibid.

189. Paul Dean, *The Report of the Dean*, Georgetown University Law Center, 1966-1968.

190. The counter-dedication arose when the Law Center invited both Chief Justice Warren Burger and activist lawyer William Kunstler to speak at the dedication. Burger hated Kunstler and all he stood for. When Burger refused to appear on the same stage as Kunstler, Law Center officials uninvited Kunstler. The activist students quickly organized the counter-dedication and obtained a permit to stage it at the corner of New Jersey and F Street, NW. The next day, with both men gone, students, faculty, and alumni participated in a symposium on the future of the legal education.

191. Coffers are decorative sunken panel in the ceiling.

192. Lord Byron, *Don Juan*, Canto I, st. 217, available at: http://www.faculty.umb.edu/elizabeth_fay/donjuan5.html (visited July 31, 2005).

193. Saint Augustine, *Confessions*, translated by R.S. Pine-Coffin (Penguin Books, 1975), 269.

194. "The Clockery: Learning Center": http://www.theclockery.com/learn1.html (visited August 18, 2005).

195. Ibid.

196. Ibid.

197. Ibid.

198. "Calendar," Encyclopedia Britannica Online School Edition, available at: http://school.eb.com/eb/article-59347 (visited July 31, 2005).

199. "Gregorian calendar," Encyclopedia Britannica Online School Edition, available at: http://school.eb.com/eb/article-9038013 (visited July 31, 2005).

200. "History of Time": http://www.allamericanclocks.com/site/626102/page/184050 (visited August 18, 2005).

201. Ibid.

202. Ibid. Merkhets were invented by astronomers in Ancient Egypt to measure hours during the night. Two merkhets would be used to line up with one of the meridians connecting the North and South Poles. Time could then be measured by observing the stars crossing the meridian.

203. James H. Breasted, *The Beginnings of Time-Measurement and the Origins of Our Calendar* in *Time and Its Mysteries: Series I, Four Lectures given on the James Arthur Foundation, New York University* (New York: New York University Press, 1936), 83.

204. Water clocks, or clepsydrae, were the only timekeeping devices available in antiquity that did not rely on sunlight or weather. The simplest ones measured time by means of the delayed outflow of water. Water would drip from one container to another at a lower height by means of gravity, and the changing water level would measure a certain time interval. Gerhard Dohrn-van Rossum, *History of the Hour: Clocks and Modern Temporal Orders* translated by Thomas Dunlap (Chicago: University of Chicago Press, 1996), 21-22.

205. "The History of Sun Clocks, Water Clocks, Obelisks": http://inventors.about.com/library/weekly/aa071401a.htm (visited August 18, 2005).

206. Ibid.

207. David S. Landes, *Revolution in Time*, 2nd ed. (Cambridge, Mass.: Belknap Press, 2000), 15- 16.

208. Ibid., 15-16, 33-36.

209. Dohrn-van Rossum, page 18.

210. Ibid., 21.

211. Ibid., 282-83.

212. Ibid., 39.

213. Ibid., 40.

214. Ibid., 4.

215. Paradiso X, 139-43; Paradiso XXVI, 13-15. Dante Alighieri, *Divine Comedy,*, ed. By U. Bosco and E. Reggio (Florence, 1979), 171, 398.

216. Robert Millikan, *Time* in *Time and Its Mysteries: Series I, Four Lectures given on the James Arthur Foundation, New York University* (New York: New York University Press, 1936), 11.

217. Dohrn-van Rossum, page 89.

218. Ibid., 120-21.

219. Landes, page 108.

220. "Clocks and Watches": http://library.thinkquest.org/20499/clock.htm (visited July 31, 2005).

221. Since the time of Isaac Newton, God has been compared to a clockmaker and the universe compared to a watch. Even though thinkers readily accepted this analogy, theologians and others expanded the concept to postulate the existence of God. The so-called argument from design states that since a watch demonstrates the existence of a watchmaker, so the mechanical, ordered, and harmonious nature of the universe demonstrates the existence of a master craftsman, namely, God. This argument is the foundation of the current intelligent design movement favored among opponents of teaching evolution in schools. Samuel L. Macey, *Clocks and the Cosmos: Time in Western Life and Thought* (Hamden, Connecticut: Archon Books, 1980), 108-09. "Intelligent Design": http://en.wikipedia.org/wiki/Intelligent_design (visited September 15, 2005).

222. Dohrn-van Rossum, pages 68-69.

223. "Clock," Encyclopedia Britannica Online School Edition, available at: http://school.eb.com/eb/article-9024419 (visited July 31, 2005).

224. Dohrn-van Rossum, pages 107-08.

225. Ibid., 127.

226. Landes, page 472, n. 10.

227. "Westminster Quarters": http://www.absoluteastronomy.com/encyclopedia/W/We/Westminster_Quarters.htm (visited July 31, 2005).

228. Ben Franklin, *Advice to a Young Tradesman* (1748), available at: http://www.angelfire.com/biz3/eserve/ayt.html (visited July 31, 2005).

229. David S. Landes, *Revolution in Time*, 2nd ed. (Cambridge, Mass.: Belknap Press, 2000), 233.

230. "NIST and ACTS": http://library.thinkquest.org/27691/trueclock/index.htm (visited July 31, 2005).

231. Anigre is a kind of mahogany.

232. "L'Enfant Plan, 100 Block of F Street, NW," *Historic Preservation Review Board: Staff Report and Recommendation*, September 28, 2000.

233. Ibid.

234. Ibid.

235. Green, vol. 1, page 136.

236. As the favorite architect of President Andrew Jackson, Robert Mills was chosen to design the Treasury Building as well as oversee the winners of the design competition for the Patent Office. He also won the design competition for the Washington Monument, although he did not live to see it completed. Weeks, pages 66-67, 76-77, 132-33.

237. Green, vol. 2, page 501.

238. Keith Melder, *City of Magnificent Intentions: A History of Washington, District of Columbia*, 2nd ed. (Washington, D.C.: Intac, 1997), 501.

239. Carl Abbott, *Political Terrain: Washington, D.C., from Tidewater Town to Global Metropolis* (Chapel Hill: University of North Carolina Press, 1999), 121.

240. The Woodrow Wilson Bridge has deteriorated considerably and carries loads for which it was never intended. As of this writing, a new bridge over the Potomac River is being constructed next to the Wilson Bridge.

241. "Hampton Roads Bridge-Tunnel & Capital Beltway Selected Virginia's Top Transportation Infrastructure Projects of 20th Century," *American Road & Transportation Builders Association*, 2002, excerpt available at: http://www.roadstothefuture.com/Capital_Beltway.html (visited September 13, 2005).

242. From 1875 to 1895, Charles Gessford was one of the most prolific residential builders in Washington, D.C. Initially a carpenter's apprentice, he ended up being most famous for his rowhouses. Once he found a design that he liked, he would replicate it down the block to create a series of rowhouses. Gessford's designs usually incorporated stone trim and red-brick rectangular projecting bays that matched the building's height. There are many stories about Philadelphia Row. The most romantic one is that Charles Gessford erected them across the street from his residence for his homesick wife, Elizabeth, so that when she looked out the window each day, she could imagine herself back home in Philadelphia. Ruth Ann Overbeck, "Capitol Hill: The Capitol is Just Up the Street," available at: http://www.capitolhillhistory.org/docs/overbeck_01.htm (visited September 15, 2005).

243. Jack Eisen, "Width and Design of Freeway Draw Criticism at D.C. Hearing," *Washington Post*, September 4, 1963.

244. Many automobile showrooms occupied 14th Street NW, between P and T Streets during this period. The elegant facades of these buildings demonstrate the elegance that once accompanied all facets of the automobile industry. These buildings are now being renovated as restaurants and loft apartments.

245. Goode, (1979), pages 421-23.

246. Major C. Wells, "Sophisticated District Freeway to Open Soon," *Washington Post*, October 13, 1973.

247. Ibid; Thomas Crosby, "Yep, It's Open... At Last," *The Evening Star*, November 6, 1973.

248. Sammie Abbott was the publicity director of the Emergency Committee on the Transportation Crisis (ECTC), an organization that opposed the Inner Loop project and frequently demonstrated at hearings. He was a "well-known anti-freeway agitator" and used his role as publicity director to the fullest. Jack White Jr., "Freeway Foes Present Case to Council," *Washington Post*, November 26, 1967; Robert G. Kaiser, "Freeway Opponents Ask Council Support; Payroll Tax Backed," *Washington Post*, December 17, 1967; Carole Shifrin, "Freeway Foes Test a Gavel Arm," *Washington Daily News*, March 14, 1968. Peter Craig was a thirty-nine-year-old transportation lawyer and as the chairman of the Transportation Committee of 100 of the Federal City, also a strong critic of the D.C. freeways. During his tenure as chairman, Craig, along with the law firm Covington & Burling, brought suit against the District for disregarding a 1893 law on highway planning. The case resulted in a victory before the U.S. Court of Appeals. "Freeway Fight Led By Lawyer," *Washington Post*, February 18, 1968.

249. The Three Sisters are three rock islands that sit in the Potomac River just upriver from Georgetown. One legend tells that three Indian maidens died at that spot trying to save their drowning lovers, members of a rival tribe, who had tried to swim across the river to join them. Another legend has them committing suicide rather than live without their lovers (members of the same tribe) who drowned in the river.

250. The most recent plan lingered before the D.C. Zoning Commission for over 15 years before is was declared no longer valid.

251. Planning Statement of the Law Center, March, 1982.

252. Ibid.

253. Forgey said as much in an article about the Law Center buildings when he noted that "Creating a memorable sense of place where there was none is one of the most important tasks that architecture can perform ..." Benjamin Forgey, "Dorm Above the Norm: Georgetown Law's Classy New Roommate," *Washington Post*, March 5, 1994.

254. Benjamin Forgey, "Georgetown Law's Happy Campus," *Washington Post*, November 8, 1997.

255. *Washington Post* architecture critic Ben Forgey describes the "Washington School" as "the interdependence of good architecture and good urban design and the importance of scale, rhythm and materials to sympathetic contextual design." Ben Forgey, Keynote Address Delivered at the Annual Meeting of the D.C. Preservation League, June 9, 2004, Tivoli Theater Building, published in the D.C. Preservation Advocate, Fall 2004, available at: http://www.dcpreservation.org/newsletter/fall_04/fall04.pdf (visited September 5, 2005).

256. Richard Guy Wilson, Introduction to *Hartman-Cox: Selected and Current Works* (Australia: The Images Publishing Group, 1994), 13.

257. Benjamin Forgey, "Dorm Above the Norm: Georgetown Law's Classy New Roommate," *Washington Post*, March 5, 1994.

258. Ibid.

259. The Folger Shakespeare Library was originally designed by Paul Philippe Cret, a Philadelphian architect who studied the Beaux Arts style in Paris. In 1983, Hartman-Cox completed an addition to the library which included a new reading room. As with the addition above the Law Center's Hart Auditorium, the new reading room had to be suspended above an area which was not structurally capable of supporting the additional load. Hartman-Cox accomplished this feat by hanging the new reading room from inverted "L"-shaped steel frames which are visible on the rear exterior of the building. "Folger Shakespeare Library: Architecture - Main Building": http://www.folger.edu/template.cfm?cid=1135 (visited September 5, 2005). George E. Hartman, *Hartman-Cox: Selected and Current Works* (Australia: The Images Publishing Group, 1994), 74.

260. *Cura personalis*, Latin for care for the whole person, is a hallmark of Jesuit education. Jesuit education strives not only to educate young people but to insure that that education is devoted to service to others. It is sometimes also referred to as "formation."

261. A reveal is a small straight-line break in coplanar surfaces that adds visual interest or adds a sense of scale. Reveals are major design elements in modern design. In pre-modern design, the designers usually put something over the seam like a piece of molding when two materials come together. The modernists solved this issue of two adjacent materials by using a reveal that held the two materials apart, thus creating a small shadow line.

262. Ernst, page 9.

263. These numbers are for the 2005-2006 academic year and are based on the number of J.D. and LL.M. "foreign students" (those without U.S. citizenship) which includes students on visas, as well as permanent residents, diplomats, and foreign workers.

264. Julia Haskel, *Shepley Bulfinch Richardson and Abbott: Past to Present* (Boston, Shepley Bulfinch Richardson and Abbott, 1999), 19.

265. We have not always considered architects great artists. "Today we are so used to celebrating the brilliance of architects like Michelangelo, Andrea Palladio, and Sir Christopher Wren, (as well 19th- and 20th-century American architects) that it is hard to imagine a time when architects and architecture were lnot esteemed. But the great architects of the Middle Ages [are] virtually anonymous... Part of the reason for this anonymity was a prejudice against manual labor on the part of both ancient and medieval authors, who assigned architecture a low place in human achievement, regarding it as an occupation unfit for an educated man." Ross King, *Brunelleschi's Dome*, Penguin Books (2000) 157.

266. Vincent Scully, Introduction to *Shepley Bulfinch Richardson and Abbott: Past to Present* (Boston, Shepley Bulfinch Richardson and Abbott, 1999), 5.

267. Commander of the Order of the British Empire. The Order is one of five classes in civil and military divisions within The Most Excellent Order of the British Empire, an order of chivalry established in by British King George V.

268. "What Will the Buildings Look Like?," *Georgetown Law Res Ipsa Loquitur*, Fall 2002, 21. All subsequent quotes come from this article.

GLOSSARY

ARCHITRAVE The lowermost part of an entablature in classical architecture that rests directly on top of a column.

BLOOM A mass of wrought iron ready for working into a shape.

BTU British Thermal Unit. A unit of heat equal to the amount of heat required to raise one pound of water one degree Fahrenheit at one atmosphere pressure.

CAMES Slender, grooved, lead bars that hold stained glass panes in windows.

CLEPSYDRA A clock powered by the flow of water.

CMU Concrete Masonry Unit, formerly known as cinder block.

COFFER Decorative sunken panels in a ceiling.

CURTAIN WALL An outer or enclosing wall, often of glass and steel, fixed to the outside of a building and serving especially as cladding.

DRY WALL A wall or ceiling constructed of a prefabricated material, such as plasterboard.

ECLECTIC STYLE An architectural style where designers selected what seems best of various styles or ideas. Picturesque eclecticism was a 19 century residential style of architecture that combined elements of Queen Anne, Second Empire, Italianate, and Federal styles.

ENTABLATURE The upper section of a classical building, resting on the columns and constituting the architrave, frieze, and cornice.

GFRC Glass Fiber Reinforced Concrete

GO CARD A digitized card permitting, among other things, the release of a locked door.

GROUND FACE BRICK Blocks of cement used for walls that have a rough rather than smooth surface texture.

HVAC Heating, Ventilation, & Air Conditioning

INTERNATIONAL STYLE An influential modernist style in architecture that developed in Europe and the United States in the 1920s and 1930s, characterized chiefly by regular, unadorned geometric forms, open interiors, and the use of glass, steel, and reinforced concrete.

JIB The arm of a mechanical crane.

LAGGING BOARDS Wooden boards placed between piles to hold back the earth during excavation.

MARVERED The act of rolling and shaping hot glass. The verb comes from the stone or cast-iron plate on which the process takes place.

MAST   A tall vertical section of a tower crane, sometimes sectioned, that rises from the base and supports the jibs and slewing unit.

MEP   Mechanical, Electrical and Plumbing systems.

MERKHET   An Ancient Egyptian used to measure hours during the night. Two merkhets would be used to line up with one of the meridians connecting the North and South Poles. Time could then be measured by observing the stars crossing the meridian.

MULLION   A vertical member, as of stone or wood, dividing a window or other opening. It is sometimes used to refer the horizontal member, which is sometimes called a muntin.

PILE   A heavy beam of timber, concrete, or steel, driven into the earth as a foundation or support for a structure.

PONTIL ROD   A solid iron rod used by glass makers to hold and spin molten glass.

REVEAL   A small straight-line break in coplanar surfaces that adds visual interest or adds a sense of scale.

SHEET ROCK   A trademark used for plasterboard sometimes used as a verb.

SHORES   Post supports holding up the concrete floor as it cures.

SHOTCRETE   Concrete which is applied with high powered hoses. It is usually used in swimming pools.

SILICA   A crystalline compound occurring abundantly as quartz, sand, and many other minerals and used to manufacture a variety of materials, especially glass and concrete.

SLEWING UNIT   The part of the tower crane that holds the gears and the motor that permits the crane to rotate to the position of the lift or the deposit.

SODA ASH   A sodium salt of carbonic acid used in making glass.

SOFFIT   The underside of a structural component, such as a beam, arch, staircase, or cornice.

SPANDREL GLASS   Black glass panes that a re part of a window system. Its purpose is to disguise beams and floors that pass behind the window.

TERRAZZO   A flooring material of marble or stone chips set in mortar and polished when dry.

TIE BACK   A steel cable that is inserted into holes drilled laterally into the soil behind the lagging boards and tied to them to reinforce the pile and lagging board system.

WALERS   Horizontal steel beams set across several piles to reinforce the lagging boards and piles.

ACKNOWLEDGMENTS

Many wonderful people contributed to the original Construction Notes e-mails and helped make this book a reality. Thanks go first to the wonderful architects and engineers who taught me how to look beyond the exterior walls of a building to understand the complexity that ultimately defines architectural beauty. My work and my life has been enriched by the architects from Shepley Bulfinch Richardson and Abbott, especially Buddy Mear, Ron Finiw, Ralph Jackson, and Carole Wedge, and those at Ellerbe Beckett, especially Kathy Alberding, Dana Hunter, and Max Merriman, and by the engineers from the Whiting-Turner Contracting Company, especially Andrew Easter, Rob Pearce, Jon Olsen, and Nick Fite. Many colleagues and friends at Georgetown also added historical and technical information to my store of knowledge, especially Peter Brown, Sherman Cohn, Abi Cruce, Matt Mantich, and Holly Eaton. My historical research was aided by librarians Abby Yochelson from the Library of Congress; Laura Bedard, Erin Kidwell, and Heather Bourk from Georgetown Law Center; Pat Tobin from Gonzaga High School in Washington, D.C.; and Margaret Goodbody, Faye Haskins, and Karen Blackburn-Mills, from the Washingtoniana Division of the Martin Luther King Library in Washington, D.C. Heather Bourk also spent countless hours helping me with photographs. My geological knowledge comes primarily from Ellis Yochelson, Research Associate at the Smithsonian Institution. My deans at Georgetown Law Center, first Judy Areen and then Alex Aleinikoff, supported me throughout the construction of the buildings and the writing of this book. Without their assistance, neither the buildings nor the book could have been completed. Georgetown's Shahriar Teymourian, who taught me to see like an engineer, Chris Augostini, Kevin Conry, Linda Davidson, Lee Thomson-Yood, and Debby Morey helped keep me laughing when both the building project and the book caused some strains. Dan Strotman, an engineer from Quadrangle Development, also guided me during some difficult periods of the project. Peter Waldron gave the book an early read, and Susan Beal did a first rate job of editing. My publishers, Paul Dickson and Doug Evelyn, and Paul's wife Nancy, believed in this book even more strongly than I did and figured out a way to bring it into existence. They could not have succeeded without the coordination by Merideth Menken and our designer, Jody Billert. Finally, my tireless, hard-working research assistant Esther Yong found things that I had lost and other things that I never could have found on my own. To all I am very grateful.

ABOUT THE AUTHOR

Wallace Mlyniec is the former Associate Dean for Clinical Education and Professor of Law at Georgetown University and was chair of the Law Center's Campus Completion Committee. That committee chose the architects for the Hotung International Law Building and the Georgetown Sport and Fitness Center and worked with them to design the buildings. Once construction began, he became the Law Center's liaison to the construction team.

Professor Mlyniec has been a member of the faculty since 1973 and is also the Director of the Juvenile Justice Clinic. He is the author of several books and many articles on children's rights, family law, and criminal justice, including *Juvenile Law and Practice in the District of Columbia*. He has been a consultant to schools of social work, to law schools, and to the National College of Juvenile and Family Court Judges. He has spoken on the topics of juvenile and criminal law throughout the nation. He is also a consultant to Shepley Bulfinch Richardson and Abbott Architects.

The author at the top of the tower crane
GEORGETOWN LAW CENTER ARCHIVE; SHAHRIAR TEYMOURIAN, PHOTOGRAPHER

INDEX

The letter "p" following a page reference indicates a photograph.